# PEELING AWAY
# THE MASK

To my children

To set you and your children
free from unhelpful ancestral patterns
and be who you truly are

Hilary Eliza Franklin

# PEELING AWAY THE MASK

*To get to the heart of
what really matters*

First published 2016 by Forward Thinking Publishing
31 Vynes Way, Nailsea, Bristol BS48 2JG

Distributor: Hilary Franklin, Highbank, London Road, Devizes, Wilts
SN10 2DS  www.hilaryfranklin.com
ISBN 978-0-9934652-1-5

The information given in this book should not be treated as a
substitute for professional medical advice; always consult a medical
practitioner. Any use of information in this book is at the reader's
discretion and risk. Neither the author nor the publisher can be held
responsible for any loss, claim or damage arising out of the use, or
misuse, of the suggestions made, the failure to take medical advice or
for any material on third party websites.

Typesetting by Geoff Fisher
geoff.fisher@yahoo.co.uk

Printed and bound in Great Britain by CPI Group (UK), Croydon CR0 4YY

Editor: Angela Clarence
Cover: Mecob Design
Proof reading: Michael Cox
Typesetting: Geoff Fisher
Printing: CPI Group (UK) Croydon CR0 4YY

# Contents

# Acknowledgements

To my husband, parents and brother.
To the father of my children,
To my children and grandchildren, stepchildren and
step-grandchildren.
Thank you for giving me the experiences that have
shown me the way from shadow to light, to truly
love you just as you are.
Gratitude to my teachers, who have held,
guided and directed me on my life path;
to my friends, students, clients,
and to all of my ancestors, who have led the way,
and whisper to me what I most need to hear.

To my husband, Norman, for his eternal love and support –
forever accepting the constant element of change necessitated
by our soul's journey together.

With gratitude to Angela Clarence, as editor, who has
mentored me through the process of editing with devotion
and expertise and always a sense of fun; to my friend Patsy
Freeman for her encouragement to keep on writing and to
Jasmine her daughter, now in Spirit, who encouraged me to
put pen to paper; and to Michael Cox for his inestimable
patience and accuracy as proof reader and brother
extraordinaire.

# Foreword by Nicola Coombe

HILARY'S LIFE DECLARES to us that the art and work of Life is a precious mystery and utterly worth the effort that authentic healing invites. "Peeling Away the Mask" is a privileged invitation from an artist to sit in her 'studio' and learn, step by unfolding step, how she made her journey, or perhaps how her journey made her. I recognised myself time and again in Hilary's compassionate hands as she describes the struggles that all of us embodied beings know well.

Hilary's telling of her story shows us how to have the confidence to trust in our own extra-ordinary self. Step by step she teaches with a firm, gentle and inviting clarity about the layers of the conditioned self, or the masks, that form us. She dares to see the symptoms of illness as guides into healing. She dares to face the endings and the beginnings of relationships. She dares to lean into systems of profound support to allow the healing of childhood trauma and to awaken intimacy. She forgives the externalised presence of God and brings herself into profound witnessing of the Truth that lives within. She travels to inner and outer landscapes and shares them truthfully and tenderly.

Ultimately Hilary inspires, in her life and through these pages, by blessing and by making visible all of the rungs on the ladder that a fully lived life contains. In the process she has become a facilitator – a minister - for profound change. May many masks be unpeeled in the turning of these pages, and may Peace indeed prevail.

**Nicola Coombe**

Focaliser, Head of OneSpirit Interfaith Foundation 15 June 2016

www.onespiritinterfaithfoundation.org

# Foreword by Chloe Goodchild

HILARY IS A very dear friend, a force of nature, a radiant and inspiring voice of truth. We have known each other for almost 20 years, during which time Hilary has become a graduate, facilitator and a treasured Friend of The Naked Voice world community.

When she chose to become an Interfaith minister in 2012 - I was lucky to witness and celebrate yet another *kenosis* and awakening in her life, that of a modern day mystic.

Hilary's gentle dynamic life's work "Peeling Away the Mask" leaves no stone unturned. It reveals the naked truth of Hilary's calling, the challenges, highs and lows that forged her commitment to the transformative power of contemplative, and creative voice, as a spiritual practice. This process, combined with her evolving life as an interfaith minister, has forged a unique legacy of love and a radiant, humble spirit.

As well as being a moving account of what it means to live an uncompromised life, "Peeling Away the Mask" reveals Hilary's role as a model of the sacred feminine, and what it means to be a woman wisdom elder in a world crying out for non-judgemental listening, co-operation, inclusiveness, unconditional presence. Hilary's book provides a user-friendly and multi-disciplinary tool-kit and guide that empowers you to discover and enjoy the undivided wholeness of your Being. "Peeling Away the Mask" reveals Hilary's commitment as wife, mother, grandmother and daughter. Wearing many hats requires immense patience and subtle activism. And it is through such complexities that Hilary demonstrates how to summon the courage and compassion required to engage with the angels and demons in all realms of our lives; whilst simultaneously demonstrating how to abide in a deepening union with the source of Life itself.

Hilary is someone who really practices what she teaches, and everyday life has been her laboratory of listening, speaking out and sharing her unique and courageous voice. Her story hides nowhere. 'Peeling Away the Mask' dissolves the old-paradigm dogmas of 'thou shalt not' to reveal Hilary's unique spectrum of multi-disciplinary practices, encouraging us all to take heart, listen, be still, move, sing, pray, surrender to our true calling, stand out and be heard. Most important, to say "YES" to sharing the gifts we have each been given to share on this uncertain, magical, graceful human journey of self-remembrance on Earth. 'Peeling Away the Mask' enables us all to unearth and engage masterfully with our own personal and collective obstacles, with a spirit of self-acceptance and self-observation that is inviolable.

Most important, Hilary is an honest, accessible and generous Heart, both as a friend and a collaborator. She is someone whom Nicola, myself and all those blessed to know Hilary - between The Naked Voice and Interfaith worldwide - can rely on to bring her kind and loving perspective, her transparency and insight, to a wide range of issues, personal and global.

Hilary is a loyal wisdom ambassador of conscious and compassionate communication. I am honoured to sing her praises and her essential call to us all - **to live an authentic life. May we all,** *Peel Away the Mask.*

**Chloe Goodchild**
Singer, voice pioneer, founder and author of **"The Naked Voice – Transform Your Life through the Power of Sound"**
(North Atlantic Books)

The Naked Voice

www.thenakedvoice.com

# Introduction

*"Please hear what I'm not saying. Don't be fooled by me, by the face I wear. For I wear a mask, a thousand masks, masks that I'm afraid to take off, and none of them is me. Pretending is an art that's second nature with me, but don't be fooled...beneath lies no complacence. Beneath lies confusion and fear and aloneness. But I hide this. I don't want anybody to know it."*

Charles L. Whitfield, MD

WHEN LLOYD WEBBER'S Phantom of the Opera first began in London in 1986 I was 36 years old. My love of music across several genres was establishing itself at the time. I longed to see it, and was privileged to be taken to the West End to see Michael Crawford and Sarah Brightman playing the main parts. I had a strange and completely compelling fascination with the Phantom and it is only now that I realise why. A scarred human being wearing a facial mask to disguise his wounding hides himself away and attracts attention by creating havoc in the opera house. As he falls in love with Christine, the opera singer who is full of light and song, she reflects the vulnerability and beauty in him, leading the audience to see his true spirit.

I chose the title for my book, or rather it chose me, when I realised that for three decades of my life I had been wearing a mask. It began to form early on in my life, when I was silenced from speaking the truth within my family. The mask helped hide my wounding and helped me to 'fit in'. My laughter hid my shame, and guilt filled me with fear keeping me from breaking free and finding the life I truly wanted. In my teens I felt like a bird imprisoned in a cage and longed to fly free, but was unable to find a way out. So I continued to fit in and follow the patterns of the society into which I was born. By early adulthood the mask had become so well established that I no longer knew who I really was.

Aged forty, my body cried out, no longer able to bear the weight of my unexpressed self. It became so rigid and stuck that I was forced to face my inner being and set myself free. Severe onset osteoarthritis was attacking my hip joints, which served to immobilise my spine and legs. Within 18 months of diagnosis I was walking on two sticks and had a disabled sticker on my car. How could I alter the prognosis that I would be in a wheelchair by the age of 60? It turns out that the illness was also a mask. Although it all felt so real, my recovery proves that it wasn't.

Many of us wear masks to differing degrees and sometimes we don't even know it. The mask becomes so much a part of us. We only wake up to reality when something shocking happens. Teachers teach what they most need to know. So it was with me.

By putting myself through various forms of Healing Arts, the layers beneath the mask began to peel away giving rise to a greater awareness of my true Self, the God within me. By seeing and listening through the eyes and ears of truth, with forgiveness and compassion, through the love which came from the depths of my heart, the layers of pain and falsity gradually peeled away revealing yet more truth, love and intimacy. Finally, I uncovered the Self which was born free, the Light that I was by birth right. The shadows that had been created by the conditioning of parents, teachers and other authority figures began to dissolve.

This is the story of how I took back my authority over my health and became a conduit of LOVE. As a result, I am now living a more connected life which serves me, those around me, and the universe. Learning the various practices which led to this healing, I felt called to share them with others. My journey from sickness to health, from grief to joy, and to a future graced with LOVE, is an open invitation to consider your own journey.

# PART ONE

Chapter One

# WAKING UP

*Through the gateway of feeling your weakness*
*lies your strength;*
*Through the gateway of feeling your pain*
*lies your pleasure and joy;*
*Through the gateway of feeling your fear*
*lies your security and safety;*
*Through the gateway of feeling your loneliness*
*lies your capacity to have fulfilment,*
*love and companionship,*
*Through the gateway of feeling your hate*
*lies your capacity to love*
*Through the gateway of feeling your hopelessness*
*lies your true and justified hope;*
*Through the gateway of accepting*
*the lacks of your childhood*
*lies your fulfilment now.*

Pathwork Lecture 190  Eva Pierrakos

A T THE AGE of forty a gift was given to me although at the
time it wasn't quite recognisable as a gift because it was
wrapped up in pain. After many months of lying awake in bed
each night with pain throughout my body, particularly in my

back and legs, I wondered what was going on. I had led an energetic life. My life had always included some kind of sport - tennis, swimming, netball, sailing and working out at a local gym. For someone who had never been ill, it was a real surprise to suddenly find my body seizing up and in such pain.

At the time I was working as personal assistant to the late Professor David Barker, a Professor of Medicine who was director of a government-run unit of the Medical Research Council, so I was in the right place to get help. I was referred to Dr. Cyrus Cooper, a Consultant Rheumatologist with whom I also worked and who has since become a professor. X-rays were taken and a diagnosis of 'sudden and severe early onset of osteoarthritis' was made. The Rheumatologist showed me the misshapen and worn out socket of my hip as well as the deteriorated vertebrae at both the top and base of my spine. He explained that he could do very little for me, apart from putting me on oral anti-inflammatory medication to alleviate the inflammation in the joints, but warned that taken on a regular basis they would inflame the lining of my stomach. He would also refer me to an orthopaedic surgeon and completed our session with the wretched news that it was a degenerative disease for which there was no cure. The prognosis was that I would be in a wheelchair by the age of sixty. The shock made me feel sick, panicky and fearful. What was I to do? How could I tell my family that they were encumbered with a potential cripple? Instinctively I played down the whole situation to protect them - so that only I would be in fear of the truth.

The pain was worst when I lay down to sleep and my body stopped moving. Anxious about my destiny I lay awake night after night in unbearable pain. I started taking the melt-in-the-mouth medication to slow down the pain and while it certainly took the edge off, it never took it away. I began to have difficulty climbing stairs and walking further than a few hundred yards. I remember the day I went shopping for an old lady's walking stick, to prop me up on my bad side. While I did everything I could to find a stick that wouldn't make me look like an old lady, I had to give in to walking and looking like somebody much older than my years. It became difficult to carry anything. I found myself beginning to be not only dependent on my family to shop and cook meals but also on strangers to carry suitcases when I was travelling. Asking for assistance was difficult for someone with such an independent nature. Although I was able to continue working as I had a relatively sedentary job. I became depressed at how restricted I was in taking part in activities with my then teenage children. Even going out for a day had to be planned, to restrict walking distances and to consider places to rest. Looking back, there was certainly an element of denial and fear from those around me about the course of the illness and at this stage I felt alone with the prospect of a serious illness looming.

The Orthopaedic Surgeon said the damage to my hip warranted putting me on the two year waiting list for a replacement, although he expressed anxiety about replacing it on "someone so young". The standard life of a replacement hip was about ten years and the subsequent replacements just five years. However, within just a year the movement in both my hips and spine had become so limited that I was unable to stand up without the aid of two walking sticks. The deterioration was frightening.

My spirit has always been strong. As a child I was encouraged to have a sense of 'trust' which came in the form of a 'faith' which my father always held. This spirit had a voice which amidst my fears and depression spoke loudly to me one day - "Go and seek alternative ways of healing yourself".

I duly asked around and was recommended to a Shiatsu Practitioner. Shiatsu is an ancient Japanese healing art which has its foundations in ancient Chinese medicine. It works with 'universal energy' (about which I knew nothing) to clear blockages in the body's meridian system - a system of channels connected to each organ and to our seven energy centres or 'chakras'. An appointment was duly booked with Diana who lived north of the New Forest. I found myself travelling down a track to a small cottage set in a huge garden containing a traditional, brightly painted gypsy caravan. It could not have been more alternative or more different from a doctor's clinic! It felt strange, but also quaint and homely. A voice called to me to come in out of the cold and I ventured up the steps into a snug and cosy space where a fire burned brightly in a little wood burning stove. Nowadays, we see complimentary clinics in every high street while twenty years ago this type of work was done in the home of the practitioner. Diana sat me down and gently asked me to tell her something about my life before beginning a treatment. She seemed to have an awareness of how to manage this body of mine, which felt absolutely wonderful. I felt nurtured and cared for receiving warmth and love from her physical touch as she massaged and stretched my body. She treated the areas of severe pain with a stick of heated Moxa herbs. The warmth went deep inside my body and radiated throughout my spine giving an extraordinary kind of comfort which I had never felt before. I had no idea what was going on, but I knew that it felt good.

Regular visits afforded me great relief from my physical pain and supported me mentally and emotionally. Unbeknownst to me the treatment was more than just physical. It was also working on mental and emotional levels, changing patterns which my body had been holding for years - the first of many layers of conditioning to fall away.

Diana encouraged me to consider my own needs, a concept quite alien to me. I concluded that as well as needing more relaxation, the hip operation was a need more urgent than anything else. If I could get the surgery done on my right hip which was beyond redemption, I could work on the other parts which were not so damaged to prevent further deterioration. I decided to push the medics for an operation in the hope that I could become mobile. They reluctantly agreed on the basis that I took responsibility for having it so early. This I agreed to do. The operation was performed and the predominant pain was miraculously removed. It was instant. Although it did take several months before I could begin to walk normally. After eighteen months of hobbling around on sticks my hip muscles needed rebuilding. Unaccountably, the doctors offered no advice on how to go about this. However, I took up swimming and worked one-to-one with a yoga teacher who gave me specific exercises designed to rebuild the wasted muscles. The power of these daily routines, combined with eating a healthy diet, began to give me a stronger body. I realised that I must instigate a completely new life path to improve my health. It also became clear that I needed to devote time to looking inside myself. My life was sacred. My responsibility as a parent meant that I needed to find a way to be well and independent. The disease was not going to go away of its own accord.

Diana's Shiatsu teachings showed me that my body was trying to tell me something, something which I had been denying for a long time. I began to realise that the pain in my body was unexpressed emotion which had given rise to physical dis-ease. I had been holding a great deal of unspoken grief, anger and resentment. It had always been difficult for me to say what I truly felt about anything. It was so much easier to hold in my feelings. This, I began to understand, had been my downfall, this withholding of true expression, always choosing to remain silent rather than create any form of upset or chaos by speaking my truth.

As my husband and I approached our twenty-fifth wedding

anniversary it became clear to me, and to him, that it was time to face the truth and let go of the relationship. We had not been at ease with one another for many years. We talked at great length, probably for the first time ever, and a mutual decision was made to sell the house and separate. Our mutual desire was to stay as friends, but to go our separate ways while still jointly supporting our children, now seventeen and twenty. Our decision seemed to burst a bubble of tension and we both began to let go and relax. It was a decision that set me on the road to freedom, freedom to listen to my own voice; to get to know who I really was outside the rigid box I had lived in for years. Yet it was a massive, painfully tough decision which involved a great deal of grief around the loss of our family unit and even now there are times when I grieve that loss.

The house was duly sold and within six months we had both embarked on new and separate journeys. For me it was to be a journey of discovery of what my mind and body needed in order to heal. Many of us, particularly in the western world, lose touch with both our bodies and our True Self and become governed by our minds and sometimes by the minds of those around us. I absolutely believe that our lives are a manifestation of our thoughts - so in order to experience LOVE our thoughts about ourselves and others need to be based on love, trust, gentleness and compassion - not on fear, anxiety and emotion.

When I was diagnosed with osteoarthritis I had been in 'survival mode', not seeing my life as it truly was and ignoring the warning signs of my illness. I think many people in society are in this mode at the moment and have been for generations - not listening to their hearts or bodies, only listening to their minds. My illness inspired me to begin by reading literature about alternative ways of living and being, autobiographies of people recovering from serious diseases such as terminal cancer, auto-immune disease, addiction, depression and mental illnesses. I learnt that it was possible to heal by changing the patterns of our lives and by finding that aspect of ourselves which is unharmed and untainted, that peace which exists within us all. I became filled with a deep knowing that I could rid myself of this disease. "You don't have to live with it. It is only a symptom of your life's journey so far. Change the direction of the path you walk and all will be well."

Chapter Two

# LETTING LOVE IN

*"Love is a state of being. Your love is not outside; it is deep within you. You can never lose it, and it cannot leave you. It is not dependent on some other body, some external form."*

'The Power of Now' by Eckhart Tolle

SUMMER ALWAYS BRINGS me out of my shell; I love the warmth of the sun and the outdoor life and I felt my energy begin to rise. After making a new home for myself and my daughter, I was inspired to embark on a three-year training course in Shiatsu at the Devon School of Shiatsu in Totnes. After receiving the treatment and seeing what it had done for me I wanted to learn to give it to others. Little did I know that it was to be a life-changing journey toward a new way of thinking which would give me new understandings about the fundamental issues of my life. The course opened me to ways of 'letting go' of old patterns which no longer served me.

I learnt about the mental, physical, emotional and spiritual bodies with their different levels of consciousness contained within our auric field (as human beings we emanate an energetic aura of coloured light which connects us to everyone and everything). I also learnt about the seven body energy centres which begin at the root of our spine and move on up the body through the sacrum, solar plexus, heart, throat, third eye, and crown at the top of the head; and those within our emotional, mental and spiritual bodies. Each centre is related to a particular physical and emotional function and when there is severe imbalance in these centres, we become unwell. We all have some imbalance most of the time, according to what happens to us on a daily basis. So if we have a mild shock one day and then recover the next, the energy within those particular areas will change. Our energy is changing and moving all of the time in our response to life itself.

Understanding the importance of physical movement to release built up energy in those centres, I practised a great deal of gentle and focussed exercise taught by my Shiatsu and Yoga teachers. As a result, my mind and spirit felt freer. I also recognised that the body has an intelligence which is far wiser than the mind and learnt to listen to it, to move it and to feed it well. I was fascinated by the Chinese Medicine theory of Five Elements - earth, water, fire, metal and wood. Gaining an understanding of the connection these elements have to the cycles of the body was the beginning of a new way of life for me. I began to feel deeply linked to nature and the seasons. I realised that the more we can relate to the rhythm of nature, the more in touch we can become with our body's own rhythm. I also learnt which type of foods are beneficial, according to our individual condition.

I began to realise that I was simply a conduit for the energy which was coming from Source/God/The Universe which I had never known before. He/She was a God who did not stand outside myself to be obeyed, but was within me, my own pure spirit, the essence of myself. The more I became connected with this energy, the more I realised I was working from what I now call my True Self, my God Self, my Higher Self, that part of me which is pure spirit, and the more I felt able to work with that energy. I felt great humility and gentleness and experienced LOVE coursing through my body, an energy coming directly from Source/God/The Universe, call it what you may. This brought me in touch with my joy and I began to make choices from my heart instead of my head. My heart opened more and more, giving me a vision of my True Self that was born without conditioning, while my human being self, with all its faults and fears, began to fade into the background.

I learnt that once we begin to lose attachment to our fears, we can relax and start to live in a much more positive way. I began to realise that when things go wrong, we are merely encountering the lessons we need to learn and that like my illness, these are gifts to help us evolve and change our consciousness.

Through the tools of Shiatsu and receiving the body work itself, layers upon layers of the 'mask' that was covering up my True Self began to fall away. Many of us present ourselves to the world with some sort of mask, which only serves to keep us locked into our neuroses, anxieties and fears about life and who we 'appear' to be in the world. Some people use drugs and alcohol in attempt to access this true self, but that way is neither healthy nor sustainable. Others continue to be locked in their conditioned selves and their pain bodies and display signs of ageing as the years go by, even becoming diseased in some way. Yet it doesn't have to be like that. Letting go of the mask, letting the layers drop away to allow in more LIGHT seemed to be paving the way to my health and wellbeing.

In the second year of my training an old friend of mine re-entered my life. Norman was a long standing friend who had lived in the same village in the early days of my first marriage and with whom I shared a love of music. We had even performed a repertoire of songs in public which we subsequently recorded. Norman was losing his wife Marion to ovarian cancer and during the final stages of her illness I was able to become an 'ear' for him to share his experience of grieving in anticipation of her loss. I was also privileged to be a witness to his grief when she finally died.

Norman's great philosophy in life is authenticity – what he calls wysiwyg (what you see is what you get). He dislikes anything false or unreal. This proved to be a great feature of the beginning of an exciting relationship together. There was to be nothing hidden between us, everything spoken, revealed and shared, however difficult.

Our relationship developed with ease, he felt like a soulmate to me. We had complete trust in one another, a love of arts, a shared wonder of nature and an interest in an outdoor life. During the passing of his wife, I was moved by how open he was in expressing himself which somehow opened my heart more fully to the joy that can come from someone whose heart is so open. Many of us have hearts which have been broken, and create a barrier to protect ourselves from further trauma. However, if our hearts are not open we can neither give nor receive love in its truest form.

In time we became more than friends, embarking on a courtship over a period of a year. After receiving the decree nisi from my husband Jim, Norman and I celebrated our coming together by choosing a cottage in the heart of the Dorset countryside, near Dorchester. We shared the fun of choosing the interior together and when it was ready, Norman and Marion's dog, Tosca, came to join us. We married in 1999 and the following year, just before my 50th birthday, I qualified as a Shiatsu Practitioner. I then freed myself from my work as a Human Resources manager and set up a professional healthcare practice working from home. It was a great new start for me. I knew that giving to others would sustain my ongoing rehabilitation from the osteoarthritis. My work was my medicine and my joy.

The Dorset countryside and its gentle rolling hills was another way of strengthening my legs as we walked Tosca on a daily basis. There was still pain at times, in my head, lower back and occasionally my hip, but I felt it was just there to remind me of how much progress I had made and to encourage me to continue my healing practices. I maintained yoga and swimming alongside the Shiatsu movement and stretches to keep the flow of energy within my body's system of meridians. The peace and tranquillity of my life was such a contrast to my earlier life and was a strong healing force working through me energetically. I began to feel better and better.

Chapter Three

# SHADOWS

*And everything that is hurt,*
*everything that seemed to us dark,*
*harsh, shameful, maimed, ugly, irreparably damaged,*
*is in Him transformed and recognised as whole, as lovely,*
*and radiant in His light*
*we awaken as the Beloved*
*in every last part of our body.*

St. Symeon, the New Theologian

NOW IN MY mid-sixties, I don't intellectualize love because I am able to feel and experience love deep in my heart and feel more and more Light, filling me up. There is a sense that I am beginning to embody LOVE, but this was not always the case.

Until such time as I met with my second husband, I had had little experience of intimacy, either with myself or another person. From the very beginning of my courtship with Norman, I experienced a love which seemed to arrive without judgement or condition. Our giving and receiving was balanced. While I had known unconditional love in my relationship with God, this was my first human experience of what I now know as love; an intimacy I had yearned for since childhood, and so completely different from my youthful idea of 'romantic' love.

You might think it extraordinary that it actually took me eleven years to fully receive Norman's love and move into a place of true intimacy with him. What do I mean by intimacy? Not a 'being in love' but rather an acceptance of who the other person is and truly seeing and feeling the beauty of the Light/Divinity in that person. Understanding that if the Light in us can see the Light in the other there is no longer any separation and we become one. Even though I realised that we were mirrors for each other, and that I could offer the same love to him that he had for me, I blocked the way by judging him, by my inability to accept him as he was, warts and all, without condition.

For so much of my adult life, I had a longing for intimacy. I had learnt that "falling in love" with my first husband didn't give rise to intimacy, and have since learnt that intimacy is not limited to marriage and romantic encounters. We can experience physical intimacy with our partners and intimacy without the same physical connection in our relationships with family and friends. In fact, it is my experience that, intense feelings can block us from creating balance in relationships and can also create conflict. I often had intense feelings in my first marriage and they would flip into intense distance – even the desire for separation at times.

Intimate relationships seem to occur where there is honesty and truth – when two friends or partners truly see and listen to each other, discover who they really are and connect on a level which is somehow beyond personality; some people call it at a soul level. However, we have to be willing to surrender the real truth of ourselves. Communication is the essence of this balance. We have to share ourselves with one another, warts and all, and listen to one another's stories.

Norman became a rock beneath me, alongside and behind me. Thanks to his patience I began to trust, to know and love myself. This gradually gave me the ability to rise above seeing his imperfections and to see the Light in him. I began to feel rooted and at home without the desire to criticise him - or run away when the going got tough, as it does in all live-in relationships. I learnt to communicate from a place of love when conflicts arose. We also worked on healing wounds around my sexuality. Norman listened deeply to my pain, seeing the darkness in me - the very cause of my judgement of him - with compassion and empathy. I also listened to his early family wounding concerning a sibling from whom he has been estranged intermittently throughout his life. This open line of communication helped me develop my communication skills and match his openness which enabled everything to be aired. No stone has been left unturned and we have shared much heartache over the years as we learnt to live more and more fully in our truth.

For almost fifty years my life had been very different. How many of us recognise the long-term consequences of our family experiences and conditioning and are empowered to revisit and clear them from our psyche and body? How many have family secrets and are holding onto buried pain without understanding that that is exactly where the answers to our recovery and wellbeing lie? How many of us have hit rock bottom and have been motivated enough to change things? My physical illness left me with no alternative but to acquaint myself with my shadow and to befriend it.

Many of us suffer emotional shock as children for one reason or another and if our response system doesn't know how to respond, the shock percolates all the way down to the cellular level and very often gets stuck there. As children we tend to deny our own pain and suffering because the ego goes into an automatic process to keep us safe, which creates denial and avoidance so that we don't have to face what has happened to us. We then become adept at living with defences and build complex strategies around that denial and avoidance.

My father's relationship with me during my early childhood was clearly inappropriate and as a result I was asked to harbour secrets "just between us". This not only shut down my communication but gave rise to cracks at the heart of my relationship with my mother. As a direct result of this secrecy and the separation it caused, I felt frightened, lost, unseen and unheard. Over time I buried it all, learnt not to feel and even disconnected from my body.

Unfortunately, when we don't own our experiences, or allow ourselves to mourn, our future gets tied up with the emotions of the past and our perceptions become tainted: "Love deserted me...Safety deserted me... and when these two factors combine, they create a sense of loss.

As an adult, these emotions resurfaced, along with feelings of self-betrayal; of betraying the truth of who I was. My shadow became so dark that LOVE and LIGHT faded into the background giving rise to disempowerment and depression. I became needy. Needing to be seen, needing to be heard, and needing to be loved - which gave rise to co-dependent relationships with both family and friends. Unable to speak of what I was feeling I was gradually shutting myself down.

*"When we hold onto our pain we create separateness, it allows us to separate ourselves from others, and somehow to make ourselves special. Separateness is the fundamental evil, and there is only one result of holding on to our sense of separateness; we cause other people pain too, in exactly the way that pain was inflicted on us."* from 'The Art of Effortless Living' by Ingrid Bacchi

That is what I did for years. I projected my anger passively by making myself right and others wrong, by threatening to leave relationships, by abandoning others just as I had somehow felt abandoned. I suffered from feelings of unworthiness, believing everyone was better than me, more beautiful than me, and that I was just not good enough. I felt not only that my voice could not be heard but also that it should not be heard. I masked my feelings with false smiles and laughter, stuffed my feelings inside and shut myself away. Like most Cancerians, I would crawl into my shell.

For those of us who have experienced trauma, connecting with the feelings inherent in our 'story' can be helpful. Although it is not possible to press the delete button to remove our experiences, we can connect with the associated feelings, acknowledge those feelings in order to release them, which enables us to befriend ourselves and move on with deeper insight. Facing and making friends with our Shadow - our painful experiences and a multitude of negative attributes such as avarice, carelessness, envy, fear, guilt, shame and self-importance is healing. Allowing the darkness to emerge, to look it squarely in the face and then let it go, lets the Light come in.

In essence, we start to heal and recover a sense of our True Self, that inalienable inherent sense of self-worth with which we were born.

It is sometimes difficult to work through this type of thing on our own and this is where my various therapeutic sessions came in to support me. My body was telling me much of what I needed to know through the physical pain I was experiencing. When I understood the connection between the emotions and the organs in the body as taught in Chinese medicine, I began to appreciate what had been going on for so many years - arthritis is a result of an imbalance in the element of wood energy concerning the liver and gall bladder, which is about resentment and holding on to anger. I had done a lot of that over the years and the energy had got stuck!

Deep listening to myself was probably the most helpful practice; it allowed the truth of myself to surface and sometimes rise above my mind. The more I heard what sat deep inside me, in both heart and mind, the more I could honour, forgive and let go of my childhood experiences in peace, and the more it allowed wellbeing to establish itself.

My own wisdom teachers have written detailed books on the healing arts I practice and they are noted down at the end of each of the ensuing chapters should you wish to access the information in more detail. I simply hope my story will act as a catalyst for change, if that is what you desire.

Chapter Four

# EARLY INFLUENCES

*"To be beautiful, means to be Yourself.*
*You don't need to be accepted by Others –*
*You need to accept Yourself."*

Thich Nhat Hanh

EVEN THOUGH I was known for my laughter and sense of fun and had friends, I didn't really have a close friend until I was about ten. I was a quiet child. I realise now that much of that laughter was a mask disguising the well of tears I was holding inside. I remember being part of a triangle of girlfriends in senior school, but I didn't feel I was 'good enough' and felt like the odd one out. I finally found a friend in Pam who I loved dearly and still do. She was fourteen and taught me much of what I needed to know in my mid to late teens. I remember her mother and father being gentle, open and kind and making beautiful cakes for tea on Sundays. It was a warm and relaxed household, whereas mine felt stiff and slightly scary at times. Even Pam felt uncomfortable with my mother. The rules and regulations of my home life spilled over into my social interaction with my peers and set me apart. I just didn't seem to be easily accepted anywhere. I wasn't seen or heard. As a result, it was difficult for me to even begin to know who I was.

At home I was part of a subtle, unseen, unspoken triangle

with my mother and father. My birth had been traumatic for both my mother and I. What I understand from the account of her pregnancy is that she had experienced such pain and illness she thought she would die. This had been caused by my embryo developing in a fallopian tube. In most cases these ectopic pregnancies are terminal, but my mother told me that she underwent some sort of surgery which enabled me to be placed correctly in her womb and so develop normally. When it came to labour she also had a miserable time which she endured with little support from the midwives or anyone else. She told me that she had felt abandoned whilst giving birth. Fathers were not encouraged to be present at births back in the 50s. What a loss for both parents that must have been.

The 50s was a time when children were meant to be seen and not heard. I was put in the pram at the bottom of the garden to cry myself to sleep. Mothers were considered to be spoiling their babies if they nursed them to sleep. How times have changed. Now mothers and fathers hold their babies much of their waking moments, giving them love and security.

Since both my mother and I had suffered birthing trauma it's not surprising that she found it difficult to be emotionally available to me. She was often angry and at times appeared to be quite unstable. The whole family trod on eggshells much of the time. My father seemed to understand her upsets and loved her in the best way he could by protecting her, but I had no inkling as to the cause. I later discovered that she too had suffered trauma in childhood at the hands of her father. Much of my mother's day was spent performing household duties, shopping and cooking. She combined these responsibilities with doing the accounts in the evenings for my father's business. Her main way of showing love was to feed us well and she was a great cook. Subsequently, eating was one of the best ways I found to give myself the love that I needed when times were challenging. I have since learned that we often eat to compensate for the lack of love our mothers were able to show us. My mother was also a good seamstress and made beautiful clothes for me in lovely, colourful fabrics. I have always loved beautiful clothes and at times have been a little too consumed with how I look.

My father had so hoped for a girl that he had named me 'Hilary Elizabeth' even before it was known I was a girl! I was to be "his princess". He often talked about how excited he had been when 'Babe' came into his life, and continued to call me 'Babe' even as an adult. When my mother went through a period of post-natal depression and he stepped forward to compensate for the absence of maternal love, I believe that it created such a strong bond between us, that his relationship with me became distorted for a while.

The extra attention I received must, I imagine, have had an effect on my elder brother Michael, who perhaps did not get the attention he needed from his father. Yet Michael and I shared a great love for each other and an unspoken understanding of the burden we carried living with a mother who was emotionally unstable. Nonetheless, Michael was always closer to Mum and not so close to Dad. He was deemed the 'achiever' of the family being academic, performing well at school and going on to university, while I took on the role of 'rebel' and non-achiever. We went to different schools and so had different friends, but being choristers together in our church seeded a musical bond. He was quite outstanding as a boy chorister. He had a natural musicality with 'perfect pitch'. He also became a good pianist and organist.

To outward appearances we were a normal stable family. I remember as a child living a simple life, playing in the garden on my own, building dens in the fields and cycling with my brother. We loved biking together to Sutton Park, now called

Sutton Coldfield Nature Reserve, which was where we enjoyed our freedom. We followed cycle routes winding through parkland, woods and marshes, past lakes, streams, grazing cattle, wild ponies and along an old Roman Road. I loved animals and we had hamsters and budgerigars. Like most children I would have liked to have a dog or a cat and most of all a pony, but it wasn't to be.

We had wonderful holidays on the beaches of Somerset and Devon and were given opportunities to try all sorts of hobbies. I rode ponies, ice skated on the lakes of the park in the winter, played tennis, sang and danced and studied speech and drama. We also spent many, many hours travelling the canals of England on the family canal boat which gave me a passion for nature. Michael and I also had a lot of fun on the boat sharing a double bunk, sleeping top to toe, giggling helplessly as we played with each other's toes. He was my 'big bruv' and continues to hold that place today.

While I had been such a free spirit, adventurous and full of life early on, the rigid family rules and regulations in an atmosphere where children were 'seen and not heard' and where outward appearances were what mattered, the mask which had begun to form around my family secret strengthened. If I became wilful my mother would lock me in the larder with the bottles of homemade ginger beer. The ginger beer and I nearly blew our corks. I just couldn't be the child my parents wanted me to be.

Happiest wrapped up in my own thoughts, I could be found sitting outside our house noting down car numbers! I did join the brownies and enjoyed helping out and winning badges. I also joined the church choir when I was seven and loved learning the hymns, psalms and chants. I felt held, supported and loved within the church community. It gave me an early connection to spirit which I craved, a spiritual connection with a God who might love me unconditionally, and to whom I prayed. Praying was the only thing I knew that might help me out of my loneliness and feelings of separateness. At school I spent much of my time daydreaming; looking out of the window and wondering why I couldn't be outside in nature; learning maths, chemistry and physics instead when I couldn't see a reason for them. I only came to life singing in the choir or on stage in the school plays when I became another character, at the same time somehow becoming more of myself.

Many of us who have heightened sensitivity to feelings, emotions, light, sound, in fact all forms of energy, are known as empaths. While there are a great many empaths on the planet, they have not long been understood and it is difficult for us to fit into any of the available 'boxes'. I certainly had problems fitting into the family box, the educational box, or the spiritual box, a problem conforming to both the rigid structures of school and family life.

We all have dreams about our purpose and what we would like to do with our lives, but many of us do not dare to trust ourselves enough to manifest our full potential. Because there was a discrepancy between what the real me wanted and what was expected of me, my education suffered, my spirit became dampened, and I think at a fairly early stage I began to disconnect from LOVE.

## RESOURCES

'Healing the Child Within'
'A Gift to Myself'
'Co-dependence: healing the human condition'
'Boundaries and Relationships'
by Charles Whitfield

Chapter Five

# FINDING BALANCE IN RELATIONSHIP

*"Next to love, balance is the most important thing"*

John Wooden

M Y CHILDHOOD EXPERIENCES not only created a distortion of what love is really all about but also upset the natural balance of masculine and feminine within me which caused difficulties in my ability to relate to both men and women. In a nutshell, there was a degree of fear in trusting, and certainly relating intimately, with either sex. My wounding was such that I didn't fully know how to honour a man and neither did I know how to receive being honoured as a woman, and at some level I was dishonouring both.

What I have since learnt through Taoist healing arts is that in order for relationships to be truly successful (whichever sexual preference), we have to understand the balance and feel the flow of the male and female energies which are in constant flux within ourselves as well as our partners. We are all a combination of both.

I believe the feminine spirit is tied up with Creation itself. It is patient, reverent for nature, nurturing and has an understanding of the unity of life and love. It affirms life and recognizes the value in individuals. It values the lives of others and allows them to command their own lives. It is giving and selfless. It is kindness and compassion, patience and empathy. It is connected energetically with water and flow. The unhealthy shadow side of the feminine is that it can become uncaring, place a low value on the lives of others, become mean, selfish, interfering and sabotaging. It can be impatient, blaming, gossiping and despairing.

Conversely, the masculine spirit is more about power, honouring the value of its own life and taking command of it. The masculine provides energy for accomplishment, possesses self-confidence, inner strength and dignity. The masculine demonstrates wise risk taking, decisiveness, focus and reason, power, force and resolute courage. It is connected energetically with power and heat. The unhealthy shadow side of the masculine has a passion for control. It doubts, becomes indecisive, inattentive, unreasonable, fearful, intimidated, angry, and displays much bravado. It takes foolish risks.

So it took me a while to understand which side was stronger within me. The balance between fear and anger in my life was often a good indication. If the masculine side was stronger I would tend to feel anger more often than fear. The great imbalance in this direction meant that I often felt unjustly treated by others. I became angry and aggressive because I had an unrealistically high opinion of my own rights compared to those of others.

Conversely if the feminine side was stronger, I would tend to feel fear more than anger. This imbalance meant that I felt I was treating others unfairly. I became defensive and fearful because I had an unrealistically low opinion of my own rights as compared to those of others.

These imbalances also played out behind closed doors in the bedroom. I am told similar issues occur in same sex relationships in one or both partners. Imbalances can come about because of ancestral patterning or early childhood trauma. Major imbalances can play havoc within the body, including disruption to the hormonal system.

In response to my childhood conditioning, the masculine energy became quite dominant. In my early adult years in order to feel safe, I needed control. I was fearful, inattentive and even unreasonable at times. I also became fiercely independent, developing an overly strong work ethic. Even though I was aware of my feminine side crying out for me to be more compassionate with myself and with others, I didn't know how to respond. I never rested my body. I was always on the go, needing to do, to focus, and to achieve, however tired or ill I became. I took thoughtless risks both with my body and in my relationships. I never took time out to look at my life and was unable to get in touch with my creative side. The internal agony and the subsequent external pain that manifested turned me into a victim. Subconsciously I was calling for attention, crying out to be cared for. By withdrawing from life - there were periods when I lay on the couch for hours at a time - I gained some of the attention that I subconsciously needed - totally unaware, like many people, that there was a relatively uncomplicated solution: to let go of the need to be perfect; to learn compassionate and holistic ways of caring for myself; and to become a loving parent to myself.

What I did instead was to give my power away to another in the hope of finding love, and then became annoyed when that person did not fulfil my expectations!

So often in relationships we expect the other person to be perfect, at the same time wanting to show how perfect we are and so hiding our vulnerability. When we can't be vulnerable with the other person, let alone with ourselves, we totally lose the connection and intimacy we so desperately desire. I know that the difficulties I have had in relationships in my life have arisen when I have not been truthful, authentic and vulnerable with people; when I have tried to be what I thought others wanted me to be. Now, when I show my vulnerability, my truth becomes apparent and the resulting connections are so much stronger because they are authentic.

Whoever we are and wherever we are on this planet, we are in relationship with others, be they mother, father, sister, brother, partner, friend or colleague.

Relationships, I realise now, are often perfectly constructed mechanisms for us to learn about ourselves, if we are prepared to work at them. My life path, this time around, has definitely involved discovering a truer sense of myself through the lens of being in a relationship. Although I have by no means mastered the art of being in a relationship, I have begun to master the task of self-love through my own truth.

So what does loving ourselves involve? Well I believe the early stages involve removing the masks that we create to cover up all the hard feelings that we have inside. Many of us try to numb these feelings so that we don't appear vulnerable in the sight of others, so that we appear to be 'holding it together'. However, in the process of numbing these difficult feelings, we also numb our JOY. Some of the methods we use to deaden the pain include overeating, drinking and prescription drugs. Another favourite strategy is to hide our uncomfortable bits behind a mask of perfection. The absurdity of this is that if we simply allowed our authentic self to be seen with all its imperfections, allowing our vulnerability to be on show, our true beauty would be revealed. If we also accepted the flaws as well as the gifts of our children, accepting that it's not possible for them to always get things right, we wouldn't be programming them to create masks. Children usually begin to mask their feelings around school age, when they are exposed to relationships outside the family, although sometimes they find it necessary to hide from the family too.

When you observe children under the age of five you can see the confidence with which they express who they are by just 'being' in the world. Little children say what they need to say and are true to their needs. However, when they start school and step onto the path of conditioning, all that natural confidence begins to dissipate.

It is helpful to stop pretending that everything and everyone needs to be perfect and start letting ourselves be seen; to practice gratitude and joy knowing that we are ENOUGH just as we are, including any so called deficiencies.

Through the Taoist meditative practices Norman and I practised when we went to Thailand, we learned to honour one another - honouring the parts that we each play, and surrendering to one another's instinctual and intuitive power. These practices deepened our relationship, holding us in a strong way as a couple while enabling each of us to stand in our power without one taking over from the other. We are still learning to be in balance within the energies of our individual masculine/feminine, an ongoing growth and development practice for both of us.

On a collective level, the historical dominance of the patriarchal masculine, which began when the Sadducees and Pharisees prevented women from taking part in certain rituals around the time of Christ, has continued within religious culture. Society has become aware of the problem and is taking some steps toward change. I believe it is long overdue for us to reassert the feminine aspect in order to achieve a greater balance. It is time to recognise and demonstrate that the feminine side has value, and that its value lies in knowing and doing what is good for society. Giving and helping each other personally, within our local communities, both nationally and globally, can bring an end to social confusion, unrest and turmoil, and create the long promised Heaven on Earth.

**RESOURCES**

'Basic Practices of Universal Healing Tao'
'Awakening Healing Light'
'Healing Love'
by Mantak Chia
www.mantakchia.com
www.universal-tao.com
www.taoism.net

Chapter Six

# ANCESTRAL PATTERNS

*"There are some trees, Watson, which grow to a certain height and then suddenly develop some unsightly eccentricity. You will see it often in humans. I have a theory that the individual represents in his development the whole procession of his ancestors, and that such a sudden turn to good or evil stands for some strong influence which came into the line of his pedigree. The person becomes, as it were, the epitome of the history of his own family!"*

Sir Arthur Conan Doyle

IN HER BOOK 'Sexual Politics', Kate Millet pronounces that "male and female are two cultures and their life experiences are utterly different. Conflict is a natural part of life and if handled properly disagreements present an important opportunity for couples to learn and grow together. A little known yet significant factor is that most of the emotional responses triggered in couples are not due to difficulties within the relationship, but were laid down in the pain body during childhood." (See Chapter 8 for more on the Pain Body). I am quite sure that both my ancestral patterns and those of my first husband presented us with challenges in our relationship that neither of us really understood at the time. Nevertheless, our twenty-five-year long relationship had a real purpose and much richness, not the least of which are our two wonderful children, Alex and Celia.

I was married at the tender age of 21 and it was quite an adventure. A combination of compromise, fun and seriously testing times, for which I take at least 50% responsibility now that I understand the patterns. Our lives together were based largely on our parents' example of marriage. Our fathers held a patriarchal position in the family and our mothers supported them in that role. Coming from a new generation, a part of me wanted to handle marriage differently, but I was not able to make my voice heard, perhaps because I was not forthright enough and as a result felt disempowered. Not to mention that men of that generation, who had been brought up in the taciturn mould of 'stiff upper lips', were ill equipped to accommodate emotionally demonstrative women. Perhaps unsurprisingly this feeling of repression, of not being able to express my emotional self and make myself heard, erupted in tantrums after which I would sometimes bolt for several days until I had calmed down – with children in tow!

It was a natural progression for my first husband Jim and I to want to continue our family lines. So after renovating our home and settling into Oxfordshire village life, which was no small task, we began to try for a family. Unhappily, my pregnancies and births were not that dissimilar to my mother's experiences. The first pregnancy ended in a miscarriage; the second involved two days of protracted labour, followed by a caesarean section. Our sweet boy, Alexander, had to undergo an immediate operation for a collapsed lung and spent the following three weeks in an incubator. On my daily visits to feed him milk through a tube it was truly heart-breaking to see him all wired up. When he was finally allowed home, the relief was immense. Our son had a future. He grew into a bouncy, adventurous toddler negotiating climbing frames at two and riding a bicycle at four. Sport became his greatest interest in life and he excelled at cricket, football, rugby, tennis, swimming and sailing. My third pregnancy also necessitated a caesarean section as our beautiful daughter, Celia, was lying back to front in the womb and the doctors felt unable to risk a normal birth given my previous history. We breathed a huge sigh of relief when all turned out well. Jim then presented me with an eternity ring saying that I had now given him all that he had ever wanted. It was the most romantic moment of our entire marriage.

The two of us settled into being parents as well as anyone, given our complicated family constellations. Two of our parents had become surrogate parents in their late teens in the absence of their fathers, and another was disowned by her family when she married.

When it was time for the children to go to school, we moved to Hampshire. Jim started his own business and called on me to help. I had no idea what I was letting myself in for and just as my mother had acted as a bookkeeper for my father's business, I found myself working alongside my husband. It was a challenge entering a business environment as I had had no actual training and it was difficult for me to leave the children with a nanny, yet it was our future and while it was hard work, it was also exciting. We had a business to run and a wonderful family to bring up. Jim and I accepted that our relationship, although somewhat challenging, was just how it was, good enough to carry through our responsibilities as parents. The children were doing well, Alex becoming more and more interested in sport and Celia in music - playing the saxophone, singing and acting in school plays.

After some three years, the business needed an injection of finance and Jim put our house up as surety for a loan at the bank. By now I was the Company Secretary and was asked to co-sign the papers as co-owner of the house. I don't think I fully understood the legal implications and I am not sure Jim did either. I just thought it was what you did when you borrowed money for a business. Unaware of the risks involved, I was shocked when the business went into receivership and we lost our home. The experience drove a wedge between Jim and I which neither of us knew how to handle and from which we never really recovered. We had lost our business and our home and had to find a way of rebuilding our lives for the sake of our children if nothing else.

The children were obliged to change schools, but as it happened Celia was delighted to move to the local comprehensive which was a much better fit for her as she had set her sights on social work. It also offered her a more satisfying social life. Alexander signed up for the local sixth form college and subsequently embarked on a year's work experience before travelling around Australia. Jim went back to being a sales agent in the furniture industry and I went to work as a secretary in a Medical Research Centre. After a while, with the help of parents, we were able to put together a deposit, finance a mortgage and buy another house. We were starting all over again. It was not an easy time for any of us.

In the interests of uncovering secrets, I wish to relate that about two years before the demise of the business, I had run into my childhood sweetheart quite by chance. It was a catastrophic meeting because we both discovered that our attraction had not abated and we were both feeling unsettled in our marriages. Lured by the promise of a second chance at love, and the prospect of a more equal and fulfilling relationship, I began an affair which led to my leaving home. I found myself commuting from Birmingham to see the children at weekends. My children have always been my raison d'être and they were miserable and therefore so was I. The situation was totally unsustainable. When I became aware of the impending downfall of the business and the possibility of our family home being reclaimed by the bank, I felt I had to return to my husband to lend my support. So within a year I was home, attempting to mend my marriage amidst the chaos of losing everything we had built together.

It was at this point that my body began to go into lock down. The medical diagnosis was clear, early onset arthritis with a prognosis that I would be in a wheelchair by the age of sixty. It was alarming how rapidly I was becoming more and more incapacitated. I reached a stage when I was in so much pain that I couldn't walk around the supermarket and was therefore unable to do the shopping. I couldn't stand for longer than it took to boil a kettle and therefore couldn't do the cooking. The family had to take over my household duties and they were amazing. It must have been so difficult for them. While I was unable to walk without the aid of two sticks I had at least acquired an orange disabled sticker for the car and was still able to drive to work at the Medical Centre in Southampton and so contribute to the household finances.

Meanwhile, my colleagues at work were deeply supportive of my medical condition and although nothing could be done to alleviate the pain, they encouraged and supported me in organising a hip replacement which turned out to be a resounding success. It was not a cure for my condition and it was obvious that I needed to pay urgent attention to my health in order to try and stem the predictions of life in a wheelchair within fifteen years.

As my son Alex approached his twenty-first birthday, and Celia was studying for a GNVQ Health and Social Care course to enable her career in youth and social work, it was clear to both Jim and I that our marriage had run its course, so we decided to sell the house and go our separate ways. Once we'd made the decision we were much more relaxed with each other, and our subsequent separation proved amicable and relatively easy. We have worked on keeping a good connection and meet on celebratory occasions every year.

## FAMILY CONSTELLATIONS

When I came across Bert Hellinger's 'Family Constellations' work, I realised it might be helpful in uncovering some of the hidden dynamics of my family. Bert Hellinger, a psychotherapist and former priest and missionary in South Africa, developed his method working with families in the mid 1990's. Now in his 80's, he is still practising and teaching his therapeutic method worldwide. The work is gentle and sensitive, allowing relationship energy to reveal itself through representatives, so that a resolution can unfold. I found a local practitioner in Bristol. Gaye Donaldson is a deeply inspiring facilitator who created a warm, safe space for our groups to explore both our family constellations and ourselves.

I see Constellation work as a form of ceremony. It can be very powerful and is done on an energetic level, guided by a higher power, without the actual family being present, creating major shifts within the real family. Representatives take on the key aspects of the family member they are representing. One 'family member' may feel anger or rage for example, and another may feel ignored or left out. It is astonishing how the 'constellation' of the family emerges during the session. A facilitator sometimes gently makes adjustments to the arrangement to see what 'feels better'. As the family constellation moves towards resolution, akin to adjusting the balance in a child's 'mobile', energetic shifts take place, and as if by magic the adjustments flow through into the real family. Changes continue to occur often for days or weeks after the exercise has been completed. Life truly imitates art through the theatre of a family constellation workshop.

Sharing stories, however difficult, goes a long way toward setting families free of their ancestral patterns which has been one of my purposes in writing this book - to set my children, grandchildren and future generations free from the unhelpful patterns inherited from previous generations. Speaking out sets everyone free.

Hellinger says - *"Unusual things happen in families and these events can affect the health of later generations without the current family members being aware of it happening. In any generation children often find themselves carrying the unresolved problems and burdens of the adults.*

*A family over many generations is like a mobile in a child's bedroom - movement at any point causes a compensating reaction in all the other parts. Children are the ones most affected by this compensatory movement. They easily and unconsciously take upon themselves unresolved matters within that family.*

*What is suppressed in a family does not disappear, but floats around waiting for an opportunity to reappear. Children feel the unexpressed energy, take it in, and live it out. And so, every mother behaves in some way like her own mother, and every father like his own father. A person who feels an inner (perhaps unconscious) connection to another family member or ancestor will often have similar feelings towards life and live out a similar fate. It can manifest as depression, guilt, thoughts of suicide or other psychological disturbance. One common cause of 'entanglement' is when a family member has been shut out, excluded and forgotten. This could be because they died very young or in childbirth through suicide or by accident, identified with a criminal or shameful event or be part of a dysfunctional family. Such a member will often be represented in a subsequent or later generation. That person could be you."*

One of the constellations I initiated around my relationship with my mother proved to be very helpful. It gave me insights into the constellation of her family, in particular her difficult relationship with her own father, her parents' relationship, and my father's relationship with his parents. The story I was given was that my maternal grandfather walked out one day, wiped the bank account clean and was never to be seen again. When my mother was eighteen she had to take responsibility for her siblings whilst her mother earned a living to support the five children. I was told very little but it was obvious that my grandfather's relationship with my grandmother was not easy, and that my mother and her siblings suffered various indignities as a result. In the constellation work I asked my 'mother' to speak of her love and approval of me. I received it within that constellation for what felt like the very first time.

It is my understanding that we choose our human parents to enhance our soul's development and growth. It is hardly ever an easy ride for any of us and the difficulties we encounter within our families often prove to be the key to our spiritual growth. Nevertheless, we are each blessed with spiritual guardians to guide us and keep us safe through the process of life, even if we are not aware of them. They are invisible to most, but I have been fortunate enough to be aware of their presence and hear their voices as they help and guide me along my life path - I call them my spirit guides and angels.

The peoples of ancient tribes relied on guidance from their spiritual guides and danced and sang to connect with their ancestors. The children of those tribal peoples were brought up with only one simple rule - to be honest in all they said and did. While most parents teach their children to be truthful and honest, they are often busy covering up lies and burying secrets they want to hide from their children. This contradiction causes great confusion in the children who tend to see straight through the subterfuge.

I know I have spent much of my life telling people what they wanted to hear - just to please or make life easy for the other person. Imagine if we felt universally able to commit to being honest in all that we said and did - particularly and especially within our own families and communities - wouldn't the world be a different place?

---

**RESOURCES**

All books written or co-written by Bert Hellinger on Family Constellations

www.hellinger.com

---

## Chapter Seven

# CO-DEPENDENCY

*"Listen to the story told by the reed of being separated:*
*Since I was cut from the reed bed*
*I have made this crying sound.*
*Anyone separated from someone he loves*
*understands what I say.*
*Anyone pulled from a source*
*longs to go back"*

Rumi, tr. Coleman Barks

CO-DEPENDENCY SEEMS RIFE in our lives as humans. In co-dependent relationships we can find it difficult to honour each individual as being different. It is difficult to see the other for who they are; rather we want the other to be as we want them to be, to think the same as us and to fulfil the needs which we cannot fulfil in ourselves. This leads to continual disappointment and dissatisfaction with the other as they fail to fulfil our desires. What I've learnt is that only we, ourselves, can fulfil our individual desires. True relationships between partners, friends or work colleagues only occur when we let go of our expectations of the other and are able to honour them as they are, while we honour ourselves as we are, in our truth.

My own response to not having my needs met by another

had always been to run away, which gave rise to loss, sadness and grief. Like many other seekers, what I was really looking for was connection, but at the time I didn't understand that this is only possible by gaining greater connection with oneself. I didn't understand that looking to others, to someone else or to an outside God to give me what I needed doesn't work.

I also gave away my power to a God outside myself, believing in what I was taught about sin. I felt guilt and shame for actions that I had been taught were misdemeanours - behaviours that had simply been expressions of my True Self.

Now that I have become more intimate with people, not only do I feel seen, heard and nurtured, I am also aware of my own needs intuitively and work towards gifting them to myself. I find myself continually receiving what I need in the form of universal assistance. Foremost among these is the sense of being loved almost without condition; a much greater sense of direction and guidance in all areas of life; a sense of balance; a sense that all is well; a sense of grace; automatic healing and peace of mind.

This guidance and inner wisdom is what supports my healing and ceremonial work, bringing the sacred into my ministerial work so that I am able to support and hold others in their times of both grief and joy.

## IN SOCIETY

It has come to my attention that humanity has also been trying to find the connection it so desires not from within but from the outside world. We have become disempowered by:

- Giving a disproportionate amount of attention to material acquisitions such as houses, cars, fashion and machines

- Considering celebrities and sporting stars to be our gods, somehow making them more worthy of being valued than ourselves

- Becoming indebted to those prepared to give us credit, rather than looking within ourselves for the wealth and rewards which we desire

- Making our doctors into gods, believing that they are all-knowing

- Allowing drug companies to dominate the world of medicine, forgetting the ancient and powerful healing properties of herbs

As a holistic healthcare practitioner, I have experienced the amazing benefits of blending allopathic medicine with holistic medicine, both for my own healing and that of my clients, including an emphasis on good nutrition by using local, organic food chock full of the nutrients which our bodies crave. I have also seen how the majority have forgotten the art of wellbeing - partly because they do not want to take responsibility for their own care, it being easier to hand over the responsibility to another. With regard to health care, I take responsibility for my own, making choices which serve my own understanding about health.

In our educational system we have given our power to the politicians who think they know best how to design blueprints for the education of our children, instead of seeking the wisdom of creative educators. We have lost all sense of what our children need to learn; of how to enable them to develop their own identities and feel empowered to be who they truly are, rather than what society wants them to be. We, the people, want our future generations to develop their imagination, their artistic and scientific talents and build their confidence so that they can believe in their uniqueness which is of such value to the world.

In the political arena we are manipulated by both politicians and the world press, who work toward creating enough fear and dread to browbeat the masses into believing that they are powerless as individuals. All these tactics are employed to manipulate our minds and control our thinking so that we willingly give away our power to the state, leaving us with a sense of hopelessness and powerlessness within our society and our world. My observations have shown me that it is only by standing outside all these systems of power and control, by choosing to live outside the box of societal expectation and by forging our own destiny, that we can individually and collectively discover love and peace.

What this has meant in my life is that I have avoided all the many systems of brainwashing which are now in place in society. Our media is the greatest source of brainwashing, so I choose to listen to the news and read newspapers infrequently. I have noticed that people who regularly read, listen and watch the news, are fearful about what is going on. Creating fear leads to mind control so that we do not think for ourselves or have individual points of view. Part, I think, of the plan to control the masses. Although it is helpful to occasionally observe the information, it is important not to associate with the fear, or get attached to the mind concepts behind it. We are seldom presented with good news!

Gathering a community of friends around me who are like-minded has been essential, particularly amongst the Naked Voice and OneSpirit Interfaith community. A circle of people with whom I can swap information and ideas and speak of my beliefs and understandings. There are many different communities developing with similar thought patterns consisting of people who are interested in World Peace, and understand that to achieve it we have to begin with ourselves and our own relationships.

Over the centuries society has also given away its power to the churches, the synagogues, the mosques and the temples, believing their truth is the only truth and that no other belief or understanding is acceptable. This has led to confusion, conflict and to religious wars. The very essence of LOVE is lost through conflict, as is connection to the True Self.

Conflict is an issue which arises in each and every one of our lives. Our habitual response is to run away from it rather than deal with it. Or to create more conflict, which leaves us with an unresolved situation, giving rise to separation within and without, breeding both diseased relationships and diseased bodies.

Although it is an ongoing challenge for me, as a result of my being silenced as a child, I am learning the importance of speaking up and voicing what I feel. It is beneficial to all parties and clears the air. It is when we don't voice our feelings but internalise them, that like blotting paper and ink, the body stores them and so we become sick. It is usually better to deal with the problem, speak one's truth in a loving and compassionate way, and attempt resolution. If we bury conflict it creates wounding in our hearts and bodies and this is one of the ways we become ill.

When we are disempowered personally, we come to a place where we feel lost and out of touch with ourselves because we believe everyone else knows best. This is a malaise of the soul and with this malaise can come physical, mental and emotional ill health. As I have already mentioned, when I was diagnosed with incurable osteoarthritis and the medical profession could do little to assist me, it inspired me to find a different way to get better and a different way of looking at life. I would like to suggest to you that there is only LOVE - or the absence of it. That it is during periods of darkness, sickness and loss of faith that we are encouraged to take stock of our lives and examine the deeper meanings of LOVE and faith. In this way we turn the difficult times, the significant hurdles in our lives, into great blessings.

Over a twenty-year period, I repeatedly asked myself "Who am I?" and "Who or what is LOVE?" and "What does my body need to heal itself?" Gradually I made what some might call a miraculous recovery from the disease which was meant to cripple me. I became free from physical pain, at peace with myself and my loved ones. I would like to suggest that this was not a miracle 'outside' the self, but rather one that took place 'inside' - a miracle that was divinely led through the wisdom of my soul. If my illness was the *absence* of LOVE, my recovery was the *discovery* of LOVE, together with CONNECTION to myself, to my husband Norman and to YOU - for we are all part of this LOVE. It is Universal.

Let us not confuse getting to know our own needs with selfishness. Indeed, my experience is that by truly understanding ourselves we can be much more aware of the needs of others. We can respect and honour them in a more authentic way and by giving and receiving LOVE, create the life we wish for ourselves and our loved ones. When we find LOVE within ourselves then what becomes important is CONNECTION to one another and to the way we care for ourselves and our loved ones - without expectation. When we find LOVE within ourselves we also CONNECT more deeply with nature. We relax and allow our bodies and our psyches to receive the life force and energy that surrounds us in the depths of great Mother Nature herself. We can begin to realize that at a greater level there is little we have to do other than learn to receive what is our right as a human being on this planet. But many see life as a struggle, believing that we have to earn the good in our life and that in order to be loved we have to please others. What we seek, love, is already there, deep inside ourselves. There is nothing to do except find our connection to it.

Many members of our society have attempted to find it by taking mind altering drugs, but I believe there is a more lasting and authentic way to discover it and that it actually heals us from top to bottom and from inside to out. In my investigations I understood this very early on - in my mind - but it was only through studying and working regularly with various spiritual practices that I was able to shift from mind to heart and really feel the difference. While I have been deeply connected to something spiritual all my life, in recent years I have had the privilege of learning what it is to embody Spirit, so that the love does not come and go with the wind, but it is there as a part of me, living through me and felt by those around me.

The biblical phrase: "Love your neighbour as yourself" has always been a profound message to me and even more so since I realised what it really means. By first being true to ourselves, we are able to love ourselves, which enables us to love others, really love others, even if we don't like them. On a collective level, it is these changes which will create peace in our world which so many of us long for. As interfaith ministers, we make a vow to keep in touch with our intentions daily. Each day my vow is *"Beloved God, I vow to uphold the spirit of truth and unity, to stand in my authority, and to see the Divine in EVERYONE. All that I am I give to you, all that you are I receive from you, for I am you and you are me."*

That is my hope for the collective too, for each one of us to see and feel the LOVE/the DIVINE in everyone, so that we can live in peace and unity. Some may think this unrealistic, but surely even having this aim is going to change something major in the world.

## RESOURCES

*'Facing Co-dependence: what it is, where it comes from, how it sabotages our lives'*
by Pia Mellody

*'Breaking Free: a recovery workbook for facing co-dependence'*
by Pia Mellody with Andrea Wells Miller

*'The Intimacy Factor: the ground rules for overcoming the obstacles to truth, respect and lasting love'*
by Pia Mellody with Lawrence S. Freundlich

Chapter Eight

# PATH TO RECOVERY

*"If we look after our bodies, they will look after us."*

Ancient Tao Wisdom

My PATH TO recovery was inspired by my two beautiful teenage children. I wanted to play a greater part in their lives. I imagined too, that they would probably have families one day and I wanted to be an active part of that. So it was vital to transform the physical pain I was experiencing and modify the picture the doctors had drawn of my being in a wheelchair at sixty. Finding alternative ways to recover my own health through holistic healthcare and a greater awareness of the way I chose to live my life had become essential. It was to be the beginning of finding myself, my truth and the love which had always been within that had so far evaded me.

## NUTRITION
The anti-inflammatory drugs the doctors gave me to ease my pain gave me gut rot, so I decided to avoid taking all pharmaceutical drugs. Instead, I eliminated aubergine, potato and tomato from my diet - all members of the deadly nightshade family which cause inflammation. I juiced aloe vera, ginger and turmeric with pineapple, which is a powerful pain relief remedy and also cleanses the system. There are also natural anti-

inflammatory tablets available at the health food store which I found useful. I gave up drinking wine, which is acidic, and began to take cider vinegar to alkalise the body. I began my day with fresh lemon and sometimes ginger in warm water. I also became vegetarian for some years, although I now enjoy a balanced diet including fish, a little meat and a great deal of fruit and vegetables, but with little dairy, sugar or wheat products.

Ever since my first hip replacement a regular swimming practice has sustained me. I also learnt meditation to still the mind, and yoga to move and stretch the body which improved my energy flow overall. Even now I have regular Shiatsu and acupuncture treatments which use the heated Moxa (mugwort) herb to warm an otherwise cold energy - usually the kidney and bladder water energy. I also found specific music with a high vibration which helped me to relax and gave me a sense of peace.

Traditional Chinese Medicine (TCM), which I studied in Shiatsu training and through the Taoist work, teaches that we are surrounded by five energy fields. As I mentioned earlier, these five environmental elements – fire, earth, metal, water and wood – each correspond to certain body organs including the heart, spleen, lungs, kidneys, liver, intestines, stomach, urinary bladder and gall bladder. The five different elements are also associated with different times of the year: fire with summer, earth with late summer, metal with autumn, water with winter, and wood with spring. The five elements interact and depend on each other. Keeping all the elements in balance promotes harmony in our surroundings and our health. By eating foods associated with each of the elements, you can promote balance in the body. Five element foods that are encouraged are: grains, tubers, beans, vegetables and fruits. Restricted foods include: meat, sugar, overly-processed chemical foods, deep-fried foods, liquor, beer and wine.

## THE PAIN BODY

Early on in my research concerning pain and illness I discovered the existence of what is called in holistic medicine the Pain Body. It is very much like the ego in that it has a lot to say for itself and can take over! It consists of an accumulation of painful life experiences - incidents that have not been fully faced and accepted at the time. These events leave behind energy forms that coalesce into a Pain Body; the emotional aspect of our ego consciousness.

When something triggers a very strong emotional reaction, the Pain Body is activated. At that moment it takes over our mind and our internal dialogue - which is dysfunctional enough at the best of times. The Pain Body not only manifests emotional disturbance but can transform into physical pain and physical illness. I was determined to find a way to get rid of it! An idea began to form that perhaps LOVE could somehow take over.

'The Power of Inner Peace' by Diana Cooper; 'Living with Joy' by Sanaya Roman; and 'The Creation of Health' by Caroline Myss were three books which really inspired me at this stage. *"What a person believes to be true about life, about GOD or LOVE, plays a powerful role in determining how a person lives. The empowering belief patterns and positive mental attitudes we possess are essential to creating a healthy body as well as a healthy life. People's lives revolve around love, and when stressful experience in relationships exists, the physical body can easily break down in response. A person who lives a life devoid of love is a prime candidate for disease." Caroline Myss*

In order to free myself of physical pain, it was important for me to become more and more conscious of the inherent Light, wellbeing and beauty within me, which I began to call the Light or the Presence. I felt my senses heighten when I connected more fully with my breath and when entering into inner listening mode. Little by little these practices reduced the effects of my pain body and the voice of my ego. The more 'present' I was with myself and with LOVE/God, the less the Pain Body could feed on my thoughts or on other people's responses. I learnt to observe it, to be 'the witness', and to give myself space, to be in the presence of LOVE itself and gradually the energy of the pain body decreased.

## ENERGY

Through the Chinese wisdom of the Tao which my husband and I discovered on our travels through Thailand, and also through the Five Element theory of Chinese Medicine, I discovered the presence and power of ENERGY. I put this in capital letters because of its significance for us all. Most don't know what it is, how easy it is to become aware of it, and the value of having that awareness. This energy is the life force which fills the cosmos, saturates reality, and supersedes time and space. I know this energy as LOVE or God and I know that it is both feminine and masculine. It is the life force which grows flowers, forms scabs on our wounds when we cut ourselves, and constantly pushes for our sense of wholeness and wellbeing.

Absolutely everything in life has life force energy and if we become fully aware of it we can choose to draw it toward us.

## BREATH

One of the key observations I have made is that those of us who have suffered a traumatic 'shocking' experience lose the art of breathing naturally. Shocks affect the autonomic nervous system and cause us to forget to breathe and this includes the shock of our own birth. As adults, if we experience a major trauma we can be reminded subconsciously of the birth shock which increases the intensity of the problem. This often gives rise to a difficulty in breathing, or even longer term lung problems such as asthma and bronchitis. It is therefore all the more important to acquire a conscious breathing practice, one in which we can fully inflate and deflate our lungs, breathing in through the belly and right up through the body to the top of the lungs in a slow rhythmic way.

Early on in life I learnt to breathe as a singer, but now that I have a more developed understanding of how to gather life force into my body through a deep breathing process, that method has been cancelled out. Yoga teaches breathing from the belly upwards, as does the Taoist practice of Chi Kung. It creates a feeling of calm within and slows one down.

## REIKI

After qualifying as a Shiatsu practitioner I began to study Reiki with Chrissie Haskett who became my Usui Reiki Master and is now a dear friend. Reiki is another form of energy healing which has its own intelligence. This means that the person channelling the energy does not need to know about the anatomical or physiological aspects of the body as the energy goes to where it is most needed automatically. It is a safe, gentle and loving way to give and receive healing. The Reiki attunements given by the Master to the student awaken the channels in the hands and other parts of the body enabling the energy to flow. Chrissie was the one who taught me sitting/meditation which woke me up to the power of listening to the silent voice within. She also encouraged me to teach Reiki to others, which has been one of my greatest joys over the past years - helping people to awaken to working with energy.

In the summer of 2001 Chrissie handed me a book saying "As you sing I thought you might be interested in this lady." It was an autobiography by Chloe Goodchild, an international voice teacher. I couldn't put the book down. It seemed that our lives had been in parallel with one another in many ways. I felt compelled to meet her and booked onto her next residential weekend workshop.

During that first weekend Chloe introduced us to a practice known as "One Breath One Voice". She asked us to make a line at one end of the large workshop space and to imagine that we were walking to God, the final walk of our lives. She asked us to take a huge breath and sing whatever sound came forth. It was an extraordinary experience taking this breath and singing my song without words, witnessed and held by Chloe and the group. After lunch, as I lay on my bed, I felt my heart opening, literally. It was as if there was a road digger inside me digging out a hole to open a door. The vibration was powerful and tears held in my body for a lifetime and possibly more were released. When I returned to the group, the floodgates of emotion still open, Chloe showed me how to sing through the emotion and come out the other side in joy and contentment.

It was an incredible learning. I returned from the course overjoyed at having had the opportunity to work with my voice again and immediately booked onto another residential weekend. The second weekend opened my eyes and ears even further to the possibilities of working with the voice in this way. When I spoke to one of Chloe's longest standing students about the possibility of doing her three module Facilitator Training, she said that she thought I would be a suitable candidate, but to be aware that "it will change your life". As I had just experienced huge shifts with the Shiatsu training I laughed quietly to myself thinking smugly that I had made all the changes I could make! What a joke that was!!!

## RESOURCES

'Anatomy of the Spirit' *by Caroline Myss PhD*
'The Power of Inner Peace' *by Diana Cooper*
'Living with Joy' *by Sanaya Roman*
'Tao of Nutrition' *by Mao-Shing-Ni*
'Frontiers of Health' *by Dr Christine R Page*
'Carol Vorderman's Detox for Life'
'Women's Bodies, Women's Wisdom'
*by Dr Christine Northrup*

www.reikifed.co.uk
www.shiatsusociety.org
www.universal-tao.com

## Chapter Nine

# FINDING MY VOICE

*The flute of interior time is played*
*whether we hear it or not,*
*what we mean by "love" is its sound coming in.*
*When love hits the farthest edge of*
*excess, it reaches wisdom.*
*And the fragrance of that knowledge!*
*It penetrates our thick bodies;*
*it goes through walls*
*its network of notes has a structure as if a*
*million suns were arranged inside.*
*This tune has truth in it.*
*Where else have you heard a sound like this?*

Hafiz (Sufi Poet)

THE FIRST PART of Chloe Goodchild's training for facilitators in The Naked Voice consisted of three ten-day residential courses over a period of two years with home practice in between. All three parts were held at Dunderry, a beautifully restored Georgian property set in extensive grounds just outside Dublin. I had no idea what I was letting myself in for, or that I was part of the first group of facilitators to be trained. That first evening, as I stood alone in the hall before dinner I was shaking from head to foot asking myself "why on earth have I come here?" Nevertheless, when my intuition calls me to places and situations, I get up and go - and experience something akin to terror when I get there!

Our days began at 7am with Shintaido movement practice to get the body moving and the energy flowing. Shintaido is a method based on traditional martial arts with the emphasis on self-development and expression rather than self-defence. This was followed by a half-hour of sitting meditation, then breakfast, followed by an hour of preparation for the day's work. From 10am-1pm we were to offer our whole self into the silence. Chloe told us "As your thoughts arise in the silence, these feelings, whether of anxiety, longing, sadness or elation are your own self appearing in the guise of a particular feeling." We were encouraged to disappear that feeling or to play with it. As the silence began to impact my system I felt wretched, abandoned and all sorts of inner demons began to arise. We were to ask "Who am I?" To answer. To breathe. To ask again. And to continue doing this until we 'emptied out'. I began by saying: "I am Hilary. I am a therapist. I am a mother. I am a wife. I am a daughter. I am a sister. I am a physical body. I am a spiritual body. I am energy. Until, to my great surprise I found myself saying "I am God." What of course I meant by that was that I was an aspect of God. Hard to believe that I had realized so quickly that I was a part of the whole, a part of everything.

After lunch we were given two hours' free time to wander in the grounds past the ancient and majestic trees and on down to a small lake where ducks bobbed about. That was when the rot set in. When I had time on my hands I became tearful and sad. I supposed I was opening to my shadow.

We were also invited to work with the sound of the SA which is the root note which grounds us to the earth, to being on the earth plane. It is the first of the seven notes of the Indian scale, which the Naked Voice uses to ascend and descend the seven energy levels of the body, and thus the seven levels of our consciousness. We were encouraged to do this for increasing lengths of time, experiencing ourselves as temples of sound so that after a while our thoughts would start to disappear. We walked around the room singing the SA repeatedly. After a while it started to feel warm and lovely. A feeling of connection with myself and with hardly any thought. As we walked we were encouraged to follow any direction the body wanted to go and to observe what part the mind played in changing direction. We were asked to observe when the mind decided one thing and the body another. We were to "accept what is" and to remember "Thy will be done" with no praise or blame and to just enjoy the observation.

In the evenings we did some sound practice working with the AUM. Chloe speaks of Sound being the inter-connective tissue of the universe. AUM or OHM is a sound recognised by humanity everywhere as the source of all mantra. The letter A focuses our attention on the external world, U focuses it inward, and M focuses on stillness. It was and still is considered by the ancient yogis and sages of the East as the mother of all mantras.

## THE HEART SUTRA

One of the greatest of the four vocal medicines for me was the Heart Sutra, sometimes called the Heart of Understanding, which is one of the most classic and sacred of Buddhist mantras. It has been translated in several different ways, but as with most mantras the meaning has to be more intuited than understood by the mind. It is about the journey of life and beyond. It is a peaceful, contemplative mantra which we sing accompanied by the harmonium. Chloe speaks of it serving to anchor our spirit in the body, heart and mind. It brings peace to every level of your life:

> Gate, gate, pāragate, pārasamgate, bodhi svāhā
> (Go, go, far beyond, far beyond the wisdom is)

This mantra somehow stabilised my nervous system, my emotions and anxiety. It engendered a feeling of lasting comfort. My body relaxed. The darkness began to fall away and a great sense of peace filled my being. Chloe told us that she had been awoken in a dream by a Buddha telling her to "Know the heart sutra. Know the heart sutra" like a mantra itself. Holding your hands in a prayer position in front of the heart area enhances the nourishment of the mantra, an action known as 'the diamond mudra' - a mudra being a symbolic hand gesture.

Another chant that moved me and helped me to connect even more fully to my Soul Self, my True Self - even more than I had during my Shiatsu training - also assisted me in recognising that although I could see and hear demons in the silence, I could also feel beauty too:

*Self inside self you are nothing without me*
*Self inside self I am only you*
*You and I together*
*You and I together*
*Will never, never die*

On day four we were invited to write the story of our life with particular reference to experiences we wished to let go; then to share it with another member of the group before ceremonially burning it that evening. After writing it and sharing it tearfully with a colleague, I happily 'let it go' as it burned, accompanied by boisterous singing and drumming full of the energy of fire. This felt wonderfully freeing. The training was exposing the 'dark night of the soul', yet I began to move into a brighter, lighter aspect of myself.

In the silence, with little stimulation for the mind, I began to see deep inside myself. Some of the time there was darkness and some of the time a very bright light. Always there was an awareness of a source of energy, an energy that was standing inside and beside me. I became aware of my True Self standing in this beautiful Presence of warmth and love. It was extremely moving. I could see that life was like a play and I was acting a part and that life was not meant to be as serious as I had thought it to be. I saw that what was real was the conscious Presence I experienced in the silence when there was an absence of doing. I felt a sense of the Sacred. "I am a mother, or a housewife, or a teacher or whatever…" was the voice of the ego. I AM was the truth of myself. It wasn't necessary to 'do' anything, it was enough just to 'be' to reach that feeling of love and bliss. I was bowled over by this realization and it led me to move more into silence both through meditating and using the chanting with movement practice. My mind was moving into stillness on a regular basis.

Like most first steps, I didn't fully realise that this was what would bring me close to a non-judgmental God who would accept me just as I am and that I would, during Module 2, become One with that Presence, Source, Consciousness, God/LOVE.

As the course began to wind down we were asked to offer something of ourselves to the group: a song, a poem or a piece of music and so I wrote my first song, something I would never have dreamt of doing before. The pieces the group performed were called 'offerings', to help us stay in the 'Presence' rather than perform from the ego, which made a huge difference to the sound. Chloe called it moving from self-consciousness to sound-consciousness and what emanates from the soul never fails to touch the heart of the listener.

It was mid-morning and the sun was shining when we all gathered at the lakeside. The lake was like a mirror offering itself to me. Water always gives me a feeling of inner peace - I could sense the ground under my feet holding me and the birds responding to the songs that we each sang and sang back to us.

### Lakeside Magic - Song
*Hear the water singing*
*Hear the water lapping against the rocks*
*Oh it is moving on, moving on, moving*
*Down from the river, down to the sea,*
*Down from the hills, down to lake*
*Listen, listen, listen to the tinkle of the water on the rocks*
*Listen to the birds, the birds are singing their song*
*Singing their song to me....*
*Listening, singing, ah my dearest one how beautiful you are,*
*How beautiful you are. The sun, the sun is shining*
*Sing to me, sing to me, and I will sing to you*
*Sing to me, sing to me, and I will sing to you.*

*Hilary Eliza Franklin*

During those last days, World Music percussionist, poet and visionary artist, Nicholas Twilley, facilitated work particularly around the subject of rhythm. He shared his mix of indigenous rhythm drumming which served to bring me back to earth, and ground me in preparation for returning home. In one particular session he presented me with a huge cylindrical African drum upon which I was invited to sit and then beat on its face. After some time, my voice joined in and something in me shifted and moved, after which I felt much more connected to our dear Mother earth.

I was deeply inspired by the power of The Naked Voice work and by the end of the ten days knew I wanted to continue with the training despite its challenges. I had met with the God within and found a connection with our great Mother. I felt a sparkling diamond in my heart illuminating the possibilities of becoming true to myself for the very first time. I was filled with worthiness, celebrating my newly found self when I returned home to be welcomed by my beloved.

## FACILITATING THE NAKED VOICE

Within a week of returning from Dunderry, one of my Shiatsu clients, who was a musician and a singer, asked if I would offer her a Naked Voice session to assist in dealing with her emotional pain, which was underlying a good deal of her physical and mental illness. This turned out to be a very powerful experience and the beginning of a healing journey for us both - one that would rid us of old patterns and issues reaching even further back than this lifetime. We mirrored each other. Although as facilitator I felt out of my depth at times, I always had a profound sense of being guided in all that we did together. The work brought up fear and anger in us both. Once she even walked out of a session because it was so tough for her to meet herself in those dark places. Nevertheless, she returned every week for five months. I was the witness and the loyal friend and felt humbled and privileged to provide that for her, even when times were shitty! We practiced the 'seesaw', one of the most beautiful and gentle of the Shintaido exercises. I teach it a good deal in my work as it is a delightful and powerful way of connecting through our hearts. As a pair we sit on the floor back to back, moving the body like a seesaw, sounding the two sounds of OO and AH, feeling the support of each other as well as feeling a connection where the bodies meet at the heart.

This early experience of facilitating clients was as much about facilitating me as it was them. My inner journey was an ongoing transformation as I broke through more old patterns physically, emotionally and mentally. It was an important time for witnessing myself. Physically I was suffering from lower back pain. The lower back relates to the human self and to physical peril, while our legs hold feelings and beliefs about support, physical, emotional and financial. The right leg steps out into the world, representing a sense of identity, physical strength and the masculine aspect of ourselves in connection with support and being supported. The left leg is the leg of the 'past' and holds memories of what we have received as well as our ability to be open to receiving from others and our ability to trust our feminine aspects. In relation to heart feelings, it holds memories of our relationships with ourselves and with our mothers and when mothers manipulate; they contribute to feelings of a lack of emotional support.

However, I was so enthusiastic about the Shintaido movement practices which were helping my body heal that I overdid the jumping grounding exercises and within two weeks I was unable to walk! As a result of pushing my replacement hip too far; I limped in pain for three whole weeks. The lesson in this was to be kinder to myself and to my body. On an inner level I was hearing "STOP, take time for yourself, you do not need to be healing others, rest and enjoy the comforts of home and your relationship with your husband." This I did and soon felt much better.

## CLEARING

Embarking on a two-month detoxification diet was not only a great pleasure but also increased my energy levels. I began to feel an awareness of divine timing and divine presence, to enjoy the little miracles appearing in my life. I was drawn to nature, to walk in the woods and by the sea. I became more aware of my surroundings, to notice and feel my connection with plants and animals. This was helped by a delightful visitor to the Dorset coast – a dolphin - with whom I was able to swim!

Feeling that I needed to align myself more truthfully with what I wanted in life, I chose to let go of a number of friends and colleagues who were not able to support my new ethos. I knew I had to speak to them authentically - not as Hilary the people pleaser - to be able to explain why I was moving on without them. It was not easy, but it felt good to be moving into my authentic self. It was liberating. There are times when it feels right to let go of people in a loving and respectful way.

Norman and I also began to clear out some of the belongings

from our previous marriages. We also decided to simplify our lives by moving to a smaller house on the coast.

## MORE TRAINING

Returning to Dunderry for the next phase of training, Chloe first encouraged me to step into the circle of thirty students saying "Let your soul sing" without a song or anything prepared, it was a terrifying yet awe inspiring moment. For the first time in my life I 'heard' my true-self at the same time as being fully 'seen' and 'heard' by others. This was another wow moment in the training and became a regular practice both within the full group and in groups of three, or 'triads'. It was the medicine we needed to break through the protection we all tend to place around our hearts and through this practice open more fully to LOVE, to the PRESENCE.

## CHANTING

Group singing brings another dimension to the frequencies of LOVE. If you have been at a live concert, you will no doubt have noticed the difference in feeling when performers harmonise together - it usually lifts the spirits. Chanting is an ancient system of singing which has been used in many spiritual traditions. Chants come from many sources and their purpose is to call us into a field of unified sound bringing us into connection with one another and with the unchanging presence of LOVE. The more we chant, the more we instinctively sit in the SILENCE which follows the chant - the presence of LOVE. We begin to know it as a field of listening. It brings peace to our body and mind which leads to a stillness and presence in our everyday lives.

The more I began to feel that Presence, the more I began to sing and move through the dark luminosity within me and the more I moved into joy. The Naked Voice is a matter of opening the mouth and letting the sound flow, without anything in the way, the singer as an empty vessel embodying and communicating spirit. The singer is not 'doing' and there is no song, simply singing. As DH Lawrence said, "Not I, but the wind that blows through me". This wind began to blow through me each time I sang. It was the wind of my spirit, it was an expression of my true-self and it felt wonderful.

There is a deep ethos of listening in this work. The practice of moving into what Chloe calls the 'Listening Field' is gained by sitting in silence first thing in the morning every day. At Dunderry we sometimes ate together in silence. It sounds strange, but it was a lovely experience. We didn't ignore people; we simply smiled and expressed ourselves through body language. It allowed us to release the connection to our minds, thus becoming more aware of everything around us - taste, touch, smell, sight and sound - all the senses sharpened. We also discovered that during the chanting, the Presence is strong, gaining even greater strength as we drop into the silence at the end of the chant. It was striking and moving. It allowed us to begin to listen deeply to ourselves and to others in a completely new way.

I began to be truly heard by the group and my teachers without any form of judgment. The sound I produced was accepted as perfect because it was the sound of my soul, not the sound of my personality ego self. This moved me beyond any other experience I had ever had. It was an overwhelming feeling of a kind of LOVE I had never known. So began a love affair with my True Self, the part of me which was like the bubbles I blew as a child, empty and yet full enough to fly up to the sky.

Every step of new awareness was helping me let go of the dis-ease that had taken over my body, yet I was still experiencing some physical pain. This is a song I wrote during the Module 2 training reminding myself that there was a real possibility of living without pain.

**Perfect Love**

Dear Soul, dear soul
What is your longing?
It is to be in that infinite circle
To be empty and yet full
Of that love, loving my pain,
Loving my body, loving my mind
Knowing each one to be perfect
Divine Perfection, Perfection
As I hear the sound of the sea
And listen to the song of the birds
As I see new growth on the trees
I feel that knowing that all is perfection
Divine Perfection, Perfection.

My voice cries out
In surrender
My heart opens
To joy, to love of my infinite self
Divine Perfection...Perfection.
My heart yearns
To be at one with itself
Giving all, receiving all,
In the name of love
Perfect love
Divine Perfection, Perfection

Bring me back,
Bring me back home
To myself, my perfect self
It is joy, it is joy, it is perfect joy
Divine Perfection...Perfection

Hilary Eliza Franklin

## SHINTAIDO

Master Masashi Minagawa's Shintaido work inspired us all. It is a little like balletic movement, allowing us to be tender and light and humorous with our movements. Even though there were clear guidelines to the structure of the movement, within that structure there was a place for self-expression. He taught with incredible joy and lightness of spirit. The movements gave extra force to the sounds we made in our core voice practices. He called the movement mudras, as powerful whether used with or without sound. I learned that by changing the shape of the way we move, it is easier to move away from the personality self; and that by following intuitive movements I could let go of the continual chatter of my mind. This resonated so clearly with me that I was soon able to look at myself through two windows - my 'conditioned' self and my 'unconditioned' self and fully realise that my True Self was indeed the 'unconditioned self. One of Chloe's chants helped with this:

*"We are conditioned, and unconditioned.*
*We are both at the same time."*

*Chloe Goodchild*

## FIRST WORKSHOP

After the second Module, two other Naked Voice trainees and I set up a support group – a 'triad' to honour one another in our work. Each time we met we would chant and then each take our space to sing for twenty minutes whilst the remaining two took on the roles of 'witness' and 'loyal friend', usually playing the harmonium to support the sound. The process helped me to make friends with my shadow, to be more accepting of myself and allowed me to see more inner beauty. It also helped me begin to speak the words I really wanted to say rather than the words which belonged to my old programming. I didn't feel the need to fill silences when they occurred, although I still lacked confidence even within this small group of three people.

The first workshop I facilitated in our Village Hall in Dorset drew twenty people. As I introduced myself and the work to the group I felt emotional and anxious. It felt like such a huge thing for me to do. However, I had done my grounding practices and the morning session went well, ending with the chant "How I Love You" both to ourselves and to each other. In the afternoon I sat them around in a circle ready to call people to offer their own song into the circle. When it was her turn, a lady in the group who had been noticeably restless and angry, walked around the group singing "How I hate you, how I hate you" to each person in turn. While I was shocked and somewhat unnerved, it was her naked voice, it was what she wanted to say, and we were there to receive her. It certainly demonstrated how the work uncovers buried emotions, usually for the better. That workshop was a baptism of fire! Strangely, most people came back for more!

I found myself spending a good deal of time alone, dealing with internal issues as they came up. I also spent time away from home with my Naked Voice Triad colleagues. Unsurprisingly, this involvement with the Naked Voice was beginning to cause issues in my married life. The work seemed to be separating us rather than bringing us closer together. Norm felt that he was losing me. It woke me up to the fact that I can get so immersed in something that I cut myself off from others. Nonetheless, some of the issues belonged to him, so I encouraged him to explore those. While I knew that the two loves in my life were perfectly compatible, I was deeply concerned for him and for myself. The situation gave rise to some physical pain and this poem expresses what I felt at the time.

**Thy Will Be Done**
*I am brought to a standstill*
*Why? I ask myself*
*To bring you inwards again, to carry you into your pain*
*The body is locked like a safe without a code*
*Unable to open or close, get up or get down*
*Feeling trapped – are these my emotions too?*
*Those angel wings are giving me the chance to fly*
*Just as I begin to fly I am knocked down to the ground*
*Where do I go from here?*
*Which dream do I follow?*
*The Naked Voice or the Naked Man*
*THY WILL BE DONE.*
*Surely my two passions could UNITE*
*UNITED in harmony with one another*
*As my witness, I hear my voice calling*
*Feeling such longing that my Naked Self/Soul*
*Touches the heart of his soul and through our different*
*and changing passions*
*We may see ourselves as ONE, not separate in any way,*
*Together in eternity.*

*Hilary Eliza Franklin*

## MODULE 3

The vegetarian food we were served at Dunderry was extremely healthy and well thought out. While my body was feeling much clearer and lighter due to the detoxing and all the daily movement I had been doing, yet I was suffering from headaches. As we were able to choose foods we would like to exclude, I eliminated dairy, wheat and sugar to see if the headaches would evaporate and as a further detox. This worked well and I vowed to maintain this regime in a balanced way. I have since maintained the wheat elimination, and I eat a lot less dairy than before. As I have a sweet tooth, sugar has been more of a problem and I fade in and out with it, but just being aware of these healthy options is helpful. Arthritis is an inflammatory condition which responds well to all sorts of dietary eliminations, not least of which, as I mentioned before, is the deadly nightshade family which includes tomatoes, potatoes and aubergines. Whilst I was suffering from arthritis I avoided them, but now I can eat them without any problem.

During Module 3 the changes in me and the whole group were palpable, both in ourselves and our voices; we were all much, much stronger. We also learnt as much by observing Chloe facilitating others as when she facilitated us. On Easter Day, one of the women talked about a difficult relationship and Chloe spoke of the need for forgiveness. It was an ideal trigger for me to begin processing feelings around my mother, through the sound of MA. A painful task but rewarded by a vision of a beautiful dove with clipped wings, representative of me, sitting on my hand. My 'loyal friend' suggested that I sing to the bird to perhaps enable it to fly. I found myself singing "oh for the wings of a dove, far away, far away should I roam, in the wilderness build me a nest, where I stay forever at rest." I continued with some Naked Voice 'free sounding' and watched the bird fly free. What a breakthrough!

**OUTCOMES**
The Naked Voice training intensified my ongoing process of 'letting go'. Rather like peeling back the layers of the onion, I was letting go of layers of myself which no longer served me, as well as opening and blossoming into a truer sense of self. It enabled me to trust life and to become more aware of everything around me. I became my own 'witness' to my life and let go of the ego self which had been so fearful. I also

developed a 'loyal friend' consciousness. So much of my life had been taken up with wanting to please others so that I would be accepted by them. Now I found I could love and support myself as well as loving and supporting others, but only when it was right for me to do so.

As the 'singer' I have learnt to appreciate the beauty of my voice, which has empowered me and helped me to believe that I am worthy and gifted to be a creative human being, giving and receiving with grace. It also helped me to understand that as I let go of my attachment to the past it wasn't necessary to know what the future would bring. I could trust in my own Light, and know that all would be well. Also knowing that all is well at any moment in time, even when the illusion of life itself is telling me it isn't. I say illusion because I began to realize that life is a stage and we are all the players, as Shakespeare so wisely knew:

> *"All the World's a stage and all the men and women*
> *merely players,*
> *They have their exits and their entrances*
> *And one man in his time plays many parts, His acts*
> *being seven ages..."*

We create many of the dramas in our lives - write them and act them out. I feel sure that when we let drop the veil of human life, our spirits will laugh at much of what took place and at many of the decisions we made and how seriously we took life and ourselves. If only we could act with that hindsight right now, it would make our lives so much easier. If only we could know that we are complete just as we are. Well – I believe we can!

Through these trainings I came to understand the importance of daily spiritual practice. When it becomes a daily commitment in our lives it sustains our life force energy, brings us into a place of deep listening as we disregard the chatter of our lives and enables us to let go of the mundane and connect with the divine. Many of us find it difficult to make a commitment to building quiet time into our lives due to pressures of family, work, and leisure activities including television! Those that live a quiet life or live alone may find it easier to set aside the time.

Allowing spiritual practice to become a daily part of my life creates an inner sacred space where I can become a witness to my life which means that 'dramas' occur less and less, leaving more energy to give to the life I truly want to lead.

I've been so inspired by the changes the voice work has made in my life that it has become the backbone of my work, both facilitating other people's healing journeys, and in my ministry. My clients have freed themselves of unwanted patterns linked to past conditioning, as well as discovering parts of themselves they did not know existed. Sound healing is a wonderful resource for self-inquiry, allowing people to discover new ways of accepting themselves - taking them through the pain of self-consciousness into a deeper relationship with themselves and others. When people who have never sung in their life before come into my room, I ask them to tell me how they are feeling, then to connect into that feeling to make a sound. Like the new shoots of spring, out comes music. I encourage them to keep going and as the soul takes over and they let go of the personality...ah...the sound grows like painting in the air and they recognise its richness as they feel themselves awakening to their soul - that aspect of ourselves we brought with us as we entered this world.

## RESOURCES
'The Naked Voice, Transforming your Life through the
Power of Sound'
by Chloe Goodchild
'The Book of Five Rings' by Masashi Minagawa

www.thenakedvoice.com
www.thenvfa.org
www.shintaido.co.uk

Chapter Ten

# BEING THE WITNESS

*"Listen to the voice inside you*
*She is waiting to be found*
*Once you've heard that sound inside you*
*You will always stand your ground"*
*'Listen to the Voice' - Thousand Ways of Light*

Chloe Goodchild

THIS IS THE skill which sets us up for personal harmony, and could be the key to world peace. When we still our minds and become conscious of what is really going on around us it precludes us from both judgemental listening and conflict. Being the witness to myself and to others has been the greatest of all the skills I have learnt over the years. We learn it by entering into the silence. My learning began with a real fear of the silence. Little by little during those hour long sessions of silence at The Naked Voice trainings, it transformed into a longing, and has now become an ongoing yearning! I now need regular injections of 'time out' to enable me to deepen into that wonderful silence.

Deep unconditional listening is the foundation stone of an inner voice and finding that voice has profound effects. One result was that it enabled me to witness myself, as I really am. It also allowed me to become much more observant to what was going on around me in daily life. In fact, it has completely changed the way I respond to life. More often than not if a conflict arises, be it large or small, I am able to take myself out of it, think about the best way forward and respond from my heart instead of my mind, which has hugely beneficial results.

Once you have found your inner voice it has an extraordinary impact - on one's outer expression. The impact of my early conditioning required me to first hear the voice inside, the one that I was denying, and pay it loving attention, before my outer voice could truly appear and allow me to communicate truthfully. I then found myself compelled to speak when I never could have done before. And as if that was not enough, I was saying what I thought and more importantly felt. I was compelled to speak my truth. This was such a new experience for me. I had been in such fear of saying the wrong thing and upsetting others, I had to almost learn a new language. We all think we speak the truth, because we are not inherent liars; but our masks very often prevent us from speaking what we really feel. Speaking up can be challenging, but I find that the consequences are nearly always helpful both to me and the others involved.

There are myriad ways in which we cover up the truth of what we really think. How many times have we regretted what we didn't say at the time - things left unsaid because we didn't have the courage to speak? I would nearly always choose not to respond when someone said something to me which made me uncomfortable or upset. I'd bury my feelings, take it on the chin, and later feel sad or angry. Much of my first marriage was spent not expressing how I felt. I would swallow my feelings which would eat away inside, sometimes for weeks, until the anger and resentment burst out in a sort of hysteria. If only I had been able to express myself at the time but I didn't know how. As a result, a kind of communication cancer developed within my marriage. Now, when I am uncomfortable about something my second husband, says or does, a voice inside me says 'speak' and I do, even though it might be easier to say silent.

It took not only the Naked Voice training but also classes in Nonviolent Communication for me to become proficient in learning how to speak up. This Nonviolent Communication or NVC was developed by Marshall Rosenberg, an American psychotherapist who designed a way of getting men to speak in a new way to avoid conflict in prisons, which he termed a "language of the heart". He subsequently wrote books and trained facilitators to offer his work globally to organizations, individuals and couples. I can recommend it to anyone who struggles to use the right words. In its most simplistic way it asks the speaker to express three things: what do we feel, what do we need, and what request can we make to sort things out? These three rules of thumb are so helpful in taking the steam out of a situation and bringing it back to a calmer place, allowing each person to speak their truth and to change a situation which is difficult for all concerned.

Norman and I attended some of these NVC workshops together to give us the tools to be able to speak our truth to one another from our hearts; to say what we needed without getting into conflict. That is not to say that we never get into conflict, but that it happens rarely because our awareness has grown and developed over the years. This sense of truth also means that we don't have secrets. We share our inner thoughts, so we both know what we feel and think about situations before they can get difficult and as a result, we are closer. As I have become calmer and less reactive, so has he. Of course I can't always maintain this way of being, but it is part of a stream of steady growth within me which is deeply serving my life.

Being a witness for others is also hugely rewarding. As

humans, we often feel that when people share experiences, we have to then compare our own experience with theirs; comparing our lives with others, rather than seeing their life as unique and our life as unique. When a friend speaks of her excitement over a new relationship, I now find myself completely engrossed in that experience, instead of getting busy making comparisons with my own experience which is entirely different, even if I don't think it is. The person then feels really heard, because I have not diverted the conversation back to myself. The result is that my relationships have become much more balanced because I listen more deeply to what people are saying to me and I am more 'present' for them when they speak, rather than thinking about my own agenda. It is particularly helpful in my work, when clients come to me to explore themselves. I am able to hold the place of the witness the whole time, listening and asking questions to prompt them into further self-examination.

---

### RESOURCES

'Non-Violent Communication' *by Marshal Rosenberg*

https://www.cnvc.org
www.nonviolentcommunication.com

---

# PART TWO

Chapter Eleven

# GLOBAL PILGRIMAGE

*"Our life is a pilgrimage with and into the heart of God."*

Anon

THROUGH THE CENTURIES, pilgrims have journeyed to sacred places for healing, inspiration and re-direction. It is often true that an outward pilgrimage is a sign of an inner journey, of resurrection and rebirth, a journey of the heart which is held in the Creator's hands. It is rooted in the conviction that life itself is a process of continual change, movement, exploration, uncertainty and challenge. More and more people are making pilgrimages in this our 21st century. The most popular destinations welcome around two hundred million visitors a year, but in reality the pilgrim path is located everywhere and never just in sacred places. A pilgrimage is often undertaken with other people because it usually carries risk and uncertainty. Not everything on a journey is neatly sewn up. There is exploration, search, movement, questions and challenge - like life.

The act of making a pilgrimage is an easily available form of increasing awareness. It allows us to develop a deeper connection with ourselves, as well as forming a deeper relationship with Mother Earth as we journey through new and exciting landscapes. Holidays are subconscious pilgrimages - spending time in a different environment, away from our normal routines, gives us opportunities to observe our lives from a different point of view. If we choose to use them consciously to answer questions, the results can be even more beneficial.

At specific times in my life I have chosen to create space wherein I can make a physical journey. Perhaps the greatest one occurred shortly after I had completed my three-year training as a facilitator of the Naked Voice.

Meditating one morning on the edge of a clifftop in Dorset, I received a strong inner knowing that it was time to go on the journey of a lifetime - a journey I had long wished to undertake. Walking home I pondered how best to propose the idea to my husband. We had often spoken of it, however financial considerations, concern about leaving our home unoccupied, and worries about who would care for our cocker spaniel, Tosca, were obstacles that had seemed to stand in our way. So I just came out with it, saying to Norman "I want to go travelling with you. To go round the world!" and he came right back saying "Let's do it."

We came up with a simple yet supremely workable plan. We would sell the car and rent the house, which would take care of finances and keep the house occupied; we were also fairly confident that Norm's younger son and partner might enjoy taking care of Tosca, which indeed they did. The timing was right for us which is probably why the obstacles just seemed to evaporate.

We decided to visit seven countries over seven months carrying nothing but a decent sized rucksack each, so that we could use public transport as much as possible. We selected the destinations by writing the names of the countries we each most wanted to visit on slips of paper and placing them in a hat. As we took it in turns to select a name, a coherent voyage began to take shape. Central America first, embracing Mexico and Guatemala for the Mayan experience; Hawaii to swim with dolphins; New Zealand to see friends and explore; Thailand with its gentle form of Buddhism; Egypt to visit the pyramids; and finally to Austria so that Norm could visit the Vienna State Opera House.

We chose 'Developing Awareness' as a theme for this round-the-world pilgrimage, with exploring 'Self-Love' and 'Non-Attachment' as conscious goals. Letting go of all that we cherished - home, work and family - we would concentrate on relationship with ourselves and with each other, exploring new and enhanced ways of being. It was also to be a celebration of my ever improving physical wellbeing - from walking with the aid of two sticks, to shouldering my own rucksack negotiating planes, trains, local buses and who knows what other type of transport. It was bound to prove challenging, because I still found it difficult to carry weight when walking, and I certainly couldn't climb hills, mountains or more importantly pyramids - I would have to leave the pyramid climbing to Norm.

The travel agent, who specialised in sacred journeys, recommended a certain route through Guatemala and we chose to pre-book our initial accommodation and one or two unusual homestays and retreats, although our general idea was to 'respond to the moment' at each destination.

## LEAVING HOME

On the eve of our departure we lay in our beds wondering what on earth we had done. We entered into a place of enormous loss. We were feeling so bereft in anticipation of all that we were about to leave behind, we could have dropped the whole thing for two pins. Common sense prevailed and we took off the next morning without a backward glance and nothing more than rucksacks on our backs.

Our first port of call was Mexico, after a long flight to Miami and another short flight to Cancun.

## Falling Away

*All that I am, all that I know*
*Is falling, falling away from me.*
*Like quicksand I am dropping down,*
*Falling, falling into an unknown land.*
*Saying goodbye my heart begins to break.*
*There is a well inside me filled with tears.*
*Is this the road to becoming the light that I am?*
*Touch me. Hold me.*
*Teach me what I need to know.*
*Hold me in your love. Stand beside me,*
*Reassure me that all is well.*
*Where is that golden door?*
*And where is the golden key?*
*It is close by I know.*
*Show me the pathway to light.*
*That I may see.*
*That I may see.*
*As I move through this doorway*
*into the unknown lands*
*I grieve the loss of all that I know -*
*that which feels so safe.*
*I see the butterfly.*
*I see the butterfly,*
*The butterfly of transformation.*
*Like a tadpole to a frog,*
*as a chrysalis to a butterfly,*
*I can see my own journey.*

*Hilary Eliza Franklin*
*(Written the night before leaving to travel around the world)*

## MEXICO

The Mayans were a highly inspired, if bloodthirsty, culture. They ran a sophisticated trading economy in precious metals and agricultural goods. They mastered astronomy and mathematics. They also performed great feats of engineering, building extraordinary cities and temple complexes, as well as vast reservoirs and canals to conserve water and irrigate their lands. Both Norman and I felt such a strong connection to the Mayan civilisation that the overall plan of where we were going had been uniquely carved out and designed by myself and a Shaman familiar with the territory.

Our Mayan exploration began at Tulum, an ancient Mayan city and port on the Caribbean coast of Mexico, an extraordinarily picturesque place with temple ruins sitting on the cliffs above a sparkling turquoise sea and white sandy beaches. It was the beginning of our pilgrimage and almost immediately we were invited to take part in a traditional Temezcal sweat lodge ceremony.

It is a cleansing ceremony, not unlike those practised by the North American indigenous peoples, believed to help cure the symptoms of many physical, mental and emotional complaints. We had been instructed to help the purification process by eating lightly and drinking only water for the previous 24 hours. Our intention was to release and flush out all negativity. We waited outside a cave-like structure noting the huge fire burning right behind it. A conch sounded along with a drum to signal the beginning of the ceremony. The Shaman invited us to enter explaining that this purifying ceremony was for letting go of past hurts and regrets as well as forgiving ourselves and others. We crawled in on our hands and knees to join a small circle of participants, some of whom chose to be naked and some who didn't. It was a last minute decision and it had felt natural for both of us to be naked. Thirteen hot stones were brought in to represent good fortune, then the door closed. The Shaman, accompanied by the sound of a didgeridoo, began to chant an Aztec incantation as he added herbs and water to the burning coals. His voice was rich and deep and it felt as if the chant itself was cleansing deep down – quite apart from the sweat which oozed out of every pore. At one point he asked us to lie in a foetal position and to imagine ourselves as new children coming into the world without misgivings – a truly effective form of rebirthing.

Responding to what was on offer in that place, at that time, we experienced a truly auspicious start to our pilgrimage.

## GUATAMELA

The UNESCO World Heritage Site of Tikal is set amidst 120 square kilometres of rainforest, where we were able to observe flora and fauna totally new to us. We marvelled at red cedar and mahogany trees, flocks of green parrots, brightly painted scarlet, blue and yellow macaws, families of bright-eyed, long-limbed spider monkeys, and ungainly toucans sporting their massive rainbow coloured beaks.

To avoid the main body of tourists, our solicitous and resourceful guide, Bernie, arranged for us to tour the famous temple complex in reverse, timing our arrival at the Grand Plaza of Pyramids at sunset. The uplifting spiritual energy was palpable and both Norm and I felt that we had been here before in some previous existence. The magnificent, geometrically perfect, nine-storey pyramids soared above us and the surrounding jungle. These nine-storey temples are believed to relate to the evolution of human consciousness. I immediately felt a correlation to the Seven Sounds of Love, one of my voice practices signifying seven levels of consciousness and standing between the two giant pyramids, I sang my heart song with complete fearlessness, which connected me to everything around me - the Universe/God/LOVE itself. After a moment's silence, I was answered by a group of Black Montezuma birds filling the arena with their unique gurgling & hollow popping calls. In the silence that followed, a vixen descended the steps of the pyramid like a queen from another kingdom. The Spirit meanings for Fox relate to increased awareness; affinity with dream work; the ability to find your way round; a call to be discerning and to be swift in tricky situations! I sang out once more as the sun began to sink below the horizon, with the sound echoing around the plaza.

Tikal had provided us with a truly thrilling experience. As Bernie led us back through the rainforest in the gathering darkness our fearlessness was tested. However, moving into the recognition that we are one with all of nature, we allowed ourselves to relax and trust, using the palpable power of 'witness consciousness'.

Four days later we were on our way to stay with a Mayan priest in the southern highlands of Guatemala, a region of mountains and valleys criss-crossed by rivers. After an extremely bumpy ride, the rickety old taxi finally dropped us at the end of a jungle track. The sun sets quickly in the tropics and almost immediately we found ourselves in the dark. We began to stumble through the eerie blackness when as if by magic we heard our names called, and three men with flaming torches appeared. Lit by their flares we made our way up the mountain and were rewarded with a hearty meal served by Bob the priest and his French partner Anne-Marie. Here we had an opportunity to discuss the history of the Mayan civilization and to receive a spiritual blessing honouring our marriage at a Mayan ceremonial cave, a place of considerable power. When Anne-Marie and I discovered a mutual passion for singing Bob suggested that we should prepare a piece to sing together as part of the ceremony.

The Mayan caves were considered to be sacred places of transformation bridging Heaven, Earth and the Underworld. They were also associated with Fertility because of their underground waterways and womb like aspects. Caves can be challenging for anyone to negotiate with their awkward and often steep entrances, uneven and sometimes slippery floors and little illumination. This one was no exception, but with care we managed the climb down deep into its heart. We felt as if we had entered the underworld as we stood in the hollow of a dripping space, amongst giant stalagmites and stalactites. I already knew that this was a cave where all sorts of magic had taken place and as I stood there sensing its mysterious power, I heard the voice of Jesus telling me that "he was always with me even if I sometimes didn't believe it...". As Bob proceeded to bless both Norm and my relationship, and his own with Anne Marie, I felt the presence of the Mayan Gods, blessing us with their wisdom, light and understanding. It was a profound experience which thrills me even as I write these words. Anne-Marie and I sang Handel's Hallelujah and Mozart's Ave Verum Corpus followed by some naked, free singing - punctuated with silences which allowed the sounds to come back to us. At this point, Norm saw the face of a Mayan god in one of the stalactites. It was another thrilling, moving and deeply spiritual experience.

During our pilgrimage to Central America we had been cleansed in the Temezcal Aztec ceremony at Tulum; felt the potency of the Mayan civilisation at Tikal; and been blessed by a Mayan priest in a sacred cave in the Guatemalan Highlands. It was perhaps the best experience of our entire world trip in this sacred country. We have since heard that many travellers avoid Guatemala because of its high crime rate, but putting our trust in our guides, we had felt perfectly safe and secure.

Travelling together with Norman was highlighting some of

my issues around being mutually dependent, as being together 24/7 can be challenging. However, our goal of 'letting go' was alive in us and my love for Norm was growing ever deeper. Living 'in the moment' definitely emphasises the feelings in one's heart when thrown together without the hindrance of day-to-day distractions. Everything feels more alive and you are able to be more present to your own feelings, to the person with whom you are travelling and to everything around you.

## HAWAII

To reach Hawaii, we routed through San Francisco where we experienced the joys of modern civilisation in the form of a spacious hotel room, equipped with a comfortable bed, steaming hot showers, an iron and a hairdryer. It was heavenly.

One of the main callings of this trip for me had been to experience the magic of dolphins. On a previous journey, I had swum with a lone dolphin and her baby in a calm bay in Sinai, which had been a heart opening experience and ever since I felt I would be happy to travel to the ends of the earth to swim with dolphins. It is a truly holy experience. Now we would be swimming with large pods of dolphins in deep water, an exciting step on my quest to experience their extraordinary energies. They are beings of pure love.

I equate dolphins with Angelic beings. They are highly evolved, far beyond us humans and have a spiritual magic which endears them to us. They bring something which we cannot explain. I truly believe that they are here as healers, representing harmony and balance. Highly intelligent and closely in tune with their instincts, they strike a balance between instinct and our reality. They are a symbol of protection and resurrection and are playful by nature, reminding us to approach life with humour and joy. I sometimes feel them around me when swimming at my local pool back in England.

It was exciting arriving on Hawaii's Big Island and I was looking forward to the gentle, loving, compassionate water energy of the dolphins, combined with the fire energy of the volcanoes situated directly behind our homestead - both powerful agents for opening the heart.

I also hoped I would have the opportunity to free myself of the physical pain and weakness I was experiencing. Carrying the rucksack was challenging my lower back, and the changes in temperature and food were giving rise to headaches. In any case it is not unusual for me to feel unwell before a week's retreat - as if my body gets anxious and needs to prepare for the changes which are going to occur, as indeed they always do.

On the very first morning, the experience I had longed for took place. Sitting on the bow of the boat, my legs dangling in the water, two dolphins appeared beneath me. I felt their energy field, filled with pure love, and tears poured down my cheeks as I was overcome with a feeling of bliss. Then we were jumping in and out of the water in tandem with a full pod. Dolphins are beings of God, there is no question. Of course, they are also beings of Sound. They communicate with one another under the ocean through sound, and communicate with humans at a very deep level through their playfulness and willingness to draw close to us. They must have such enormous hearts as they are so completely filled up with love. They are also intergalactic beings of telepathic communication, always working as a group themselves and whenever we humans are amongst them transformation abounds within us.

By the end of the day the pain in my head was releasing and clearing, and although the headaches continued into the next day, the pain gradually lifted as I spent more time swimming with huge pods of dolphins in the flow of the tide. Then we attended a ceremony of sound with AKA, a native Hawaiian healer who skilfully played her drum into our bodies. By the end of the day the pain was gone. Something had shifted.

After a week of extremely strenuous swimming, we relaxed on the island of Kauai for a few days. Renowned for its beautiful forests and waterfalls which often feature in Hollywood movies. We gave ourselves an easy time, touring the island in a rented car and simply watching the big surf rolling onto the beaches. The American diet - heavy on meat, light on vegetables, with a lacing of sugar on so many of the foods - was something of a trial, and we were thankful to be moving on to New Zealand.

## NEW ZEALAND SOUTH ISLAND

It was Christmas when we arrived on the South Island and we had arranged to spend it spent with old friends. It was lovely to be greeted by friendly faces, to stay in their gorgeous home and meet their pet llamas - such pretty, intelligent and affectionate animals. I was totally won over by the New Zealand landscape, the vastness of the space, the size of the trees, the miles of open space with no sign of civilisation. It was like sitting in front of a huge cinema screen that had come alive, demonstrating the splendour of nature on a grand scale.

On a visit to the local hot springs, soaking and relaxing in the healing, sultry water, both Norm and I concurred that the journey was not so much about the places we were visiting but the way in which we were approaching them - conscious of our journeys within and with each other. An extraordinary opportunity for us to develop our relationship as partners, learning to be together, *"to have spaces in our togetherness, loving one another but making not a bond of love, letting the relationship be a moving sea between the shores of our souls, filling each other's cup by drinking not from the same cup, giving one another our bread, but eating not from the same loaf; not giving our hearts into each other's keeping, for only the hand of life can contain our hearts."* words spoken at our marriage ceremony drawn from 'The Prophet' by Khalil Gibran.

Meanwhile, the Tsunami which hit the Indian and Asian countries on Boxing Day killing hundreds of thousands of local people and tourists, was vibrating through the world. This was certainly a wake-up call displaying the power of nature and the fragility of life.

## SWAMI MUKTI

We heard that there was to be a 'Celebration of Sound' Voice Work Course at a retreat run by a sound expert, Swami Muktidharma, a South American. The synchronicity of this event was the only incentive I needed to persuade Norm that we should travel to the far North of the South Island for a five-day immersion into what would certainly nourish my soul and at the same time give us both some time out from one another which was bound to be good, for this being together 24/7 was intensive at times!

The accommodation was stunning. It consisted of a straw bale house in the woods overlooking Golden Bay. It was without a doubt the most beautiful accommodation we had encountered since the beginning of our travels, which was fortuitous as Norman was unwell. It was an ideal location for him to rest and recuperate.

Meanwhile, my days began at 5 a.m. and did not finish until 9 p.m. Swami Mukti was deeply inspiring, perhaps one of the greatest teachers I had come across so far. Born in Colombia, South America, he had spent half a lifetime studying with one of the great Yogis and Tantric masters, Paramahansa Satyananda, in the Bihar Yoga Tradition in North East India.

Our work included:

- Sound teachings and exercises, which felt very familiar

to me because they were based on two of the main practices of the Naked Voice.

- Karma Yoga, which is about recognising mental states working within a community, group or family. Efficiency, Equanimity, and Absence of Expectation, Egoless, Renunciation, and Conversion of Negative into Positive.

- Nadanusandhana Dharana or 'Chasing the Inner Sounds', a simple exercise that only involves putting your fingers in your ears, humming, and listening to the sound you are making, which totally shuts out the outer world. Eventually it's possible to hear the subtle sounds of the movements of your own consciousness. You can hear the whole universe in the form of sound.

- Yoga Nidra is a sense withdrawal technique that provides vitality equivalent to two hours of deep sleep and is a true tonic for the nervous system. It is a powerful method for reshaping the personality as well as promoting direction in your life along positive lines. The purpose is to create strength in the structure of the mind, rather than fulfil desires, particularly if joined with an affirmation to overcome a weakness which might be affecting your life. For example, "I am expressing the positive nature of my inner voice" or "I am developing new eating habits." As Swami Sivananda says: "Sow a thought and reap an action; Sow an action and reap a habit; Sow a habit and reap a character; Sow a character and reap a destiny." Readily available on mp3 recordings, I heartily recommend it as a form of simple meditation.

Being in the presence of such an evolved being as Mukti was indeed a gift. He told me in a private meeting that I must 'Walk My Talk', that I was to be a profound teacher, and that many people would come to me, but for now I needed to work hard and execute the practices to experience the changes in consciousness they can achieve. He also assured me that my worries and mind talk would dissipate once expansion began to take place within me. I realised that in order to progress I must practice, practice, and practice.

One of the highlights was a Kirtan evening of unbroken sound, singing Indian chants in a devotional way from the heart. Swami Mukti with his remarkable voice got totally lost in his sound, with us repeating each line that he sang, accompanied by drums and harmonium. The energy in the temple was so intense it almost crackled. The week came to a close with a Fire Ceremony, honouring our past lessons and letting go of old beliefs or patterns by writing them down and placing them in the fire before singing a mantra one hundred and eight times...quite some purification Ceremony!!

You may be wondering why so many ceremonies? These ancient earth based religions have ceremony as their basis; where we have worship they have ceremony, always communing with the nature spirits and what they often call the Great Spirit, meaning God.

### NEW ZEALAND NORTH ISLAND

Norm and I proceeded to take the ferry over to North Island and picked up a Campervan, which gave us the freedom to travel wherever we wanted and enjoy all that this magnificent country had to offer. We travelled to Waipiri beach to see the surf rollers; met with a Maori healer in Auckland; steeped ourselves in sacred Maori culture at Rotorua and Waitomo and also marvelling at the geothermal volcanic springs; at Okere

Falls on Lake Waiti we enjoyed seeing Maori tribal dancing, boiling mud pools, and geysers which spew hot water thirty feet into the air.

## BLACK WATER RAFTING

A major highlight was 'Black Water Rafting' through the Waitomo caves on the West Coast. This somewhat bold exploit was to satisfy my adventurous spirit, as well as providing an opportunity to overcome my lingering claustrophobia and awful fear of caves. Norm readily agreed to accompany me despite his misgivings. The trip involved a combination of walking, climbing, negotiating waterfalls and floating along an underground river. As we signed the liability release forms, it occurred to me that if my family could see me now they would probably think I was completely mad! I often ask myself why I never take the easy route, but something always persuades me to meet challenges head on and face my fears.

Our group of twelve travellers and two guides donned heavy wetsuits, white wellington boots and crash helmets with headlamps. After an hour-long practice drill, we were instructed on the importance of team work before choosing our black rubber rings for the deep water. I was shocked by my first glimpse of the cave entrance. It was a slit in the rock just wide enough for us to squeeze through sideways. What lay in store beyond? We found ourselves in a largish circular area where we proceeded to sit down in a circle and introduce ourselves, creating group energy - essential to aid us on our passage through the series of caves.

The cave ceiling heights varied tremendously over the two-hour trek. We walked in crocodile formation, helmet lamps illuminating our way, and our cumbersome black rubber tubes draped over one arm. I dropped mine at one point and it rapidly floated off and a member of the group kindly rescued it for me. On reaching a small waterfall, most of the group jumped off into their rubber tubes. Mindful of my hip replacement, I opted for clambering down the edge before clambering into my own tube. A favourite and delightful event occurred when we all turned off our lights to enjoy a multitude of glow worms transforming one of the caves into a magical fairyland. After that I relaxed a little more and actually began to enjoy the experience. Where the underground river ran deep, we sat into our tubes, put our feet up onto the tube of the person in front, and held onto the feet of the person behind. Fourteen adventurers linked together engendered such amazing teamwork and warmth of feeling - of security, love and oneness - I could have remained in that group forever, it felt so good.

When we climbed out of the cave into the sunlight, feelings of ecstasy swept over me. "I've done it, I've done it!" I cried. A great sense of achievement washed over me as Norm hugged and congratulated me. I had overcome my fear of being in enclosed spaces. I thanked all those who had guided me - both earth and spirit angels. Norm and I both felt that the universe had guided us to work this one out together and both admitted to each other that neither would have done it without the other. What a blessing it was to have these moments to test our spirits and our trust, and have fun all at the same time.

## THE CROWN CHAKRA OF THE WORLD
The second highlight was visiting Cape Reinga - the Land of the White Sands where two seas meet. The Maori healer, with whom I had a pre-arranged meeting at the top of a mountain, had told me it was called 'Spirit Bay' because it is a doorway through which many spirits pass during the process of death. It was this healer's task to assist in the process and he explained it was a particularly busy time because of the recent Tsunami.

He gave me his blessing and I felt truly honoured to meet with this man, who had opened his heart and told me such secrets.

Cape Reinga is considered to be the Crown Chakra of the world. The Maori guide who escorted us there in his four-wheel drive, bumping along a rough and bouncy road, exhorted us to neither eat nor drink, and to behave as we would when entering a church. We reached a hilly point of land that extends into the sea and is marked by a lighthouse, where most of the tourists congregate. However, I found and followed a small path leading lower down the hill, and discovered a secluded spot where I could connect with the energies in peace and quiet. I was so honoured and extremely moved to discover myself in this sacred place that I found myself singing; singing to all the souls, and to the world. Below me the Tasman Sea and the Pacific Ocean were coming together as walls of energy, the blue and the green, the male and the female, each with their different minerals and elements meeting and then passing through one another and becoming ONE. I felt the power of it radiate through my entire body. This image of Cape Reinga visits me now on a regular basis. It was and is extraordinary. We loved this place so much, we even dreamt of buying a plot of land there.

Driving along '90 Mile Beach' which is almost half-a-mile wide and sixty miles long was another experience of a lifetime. As our Maori guide propelled us through the vast open space, it felt so freeing and it seemed as if it might never end. As we drove, a message kept calling: *"See your life as this open pathway free of any obstacles, follow that without fear, seeing only joy and love along the way. You do not need to see ahead of you beyond today and now. See the beauty in not seeing where you are beyond the NOW."*

Norm and I were both feeling sure-footed and empowered. I was also free of the deep homesickness I had been suffering, my co-dependence issues, and had begun to sleep through the nights. I had a sense of being more in my power, more at home with myself and more comfortable with getting my personal needs met. At the same time, I felt great love for everyone, and most of all for my partner, Norm. I felt as though I could have carried on travelling for ever.

## THAILAND
In Thailand, I centred more into my heart, cleansing and opening to my vulnerability and feeling great love, compassion and gentleness. I had a longing to be exposed to Buddhism more fully, and to learn more of its ways and its outer beauty. When I had started to lose heart with the traditional dogma and patriarchy within the Christian church, one of the faiths that appealed to me was Buddhism. The gentleness of being amongst Buddhists had offered me peace, and their emphasis on an inner journey had always spoken to me.

## HEALTH SPA
After the substantial mileage we had travelled in New Zealand, we planned to chill out at a Health Spa on the island of Koh Samui. The beach bungalow accommodation was certainly not luxurious, but we were happy with it and the people running the spa were delightful. Their attitude to 'service' was performed with such grace, as taught in the Buddhist faith, that it overwhelmed us at first - something we are not entirely used to in Britain.

We walked the glorious beach in the early mornings, watching the fisherman casting their nets, and rested for a few days. I then chose to embark on a nine-day cleanse and fast. Norm chose to take instruction in Thai massage instead, which was to be a great bonus for me! He took his meals at the restaurant on the beach, run by a Chef trained in nutrition who produced healthy meals, individually cooked and presented with great love. The results were mouth-watering. Meanwhile, I was on a regimen of ginger tea, thin vegetable broth once or twice a day, vitamins and herbs to support the body, as well as water and other juices. What with meditation, yoga, a massage from Norm and colonic irrigations, the days passed swiftly by. On day three I had already begun to feel cleaner inside, and by the end of the process I had lost twelve pounds. On day ten I was allowed a papaya in the morning and a carrot and celery at lunch, followed by steamed vegetables at night. Quite a treat! It was a process and a learning that I knew I would carry forward and use again, although in hindsight, this particular regimen had been a little extreme.

One afternoon, while sitting peacefully in the bungalow during the heat of the day, I heard a loud bang - the type of sound synonymous with a car accident. I was running toward the road when I heard the manager of the spa cry out "call an ambulance". By the time I reached the scene, hundreds of Thais were lining either side of the very busy main road, in the centre of which lay an unconscious young man with blood pouring from his head. The manager's wife and I moved to his side and 'held him in light' while we mentally worked on his energy field. I found myself automatically singing the Seven Sounds of Love. We stood there in the middle of the road with people directing traffic around us until, after about ten minutes, his breath, which at times had seemed to stop completely, grew stronger and his chest moved up and down more fully. The ambulance, which was no more than an open-backed, glorified truck, arrived to take him away. As we departed the scene, not knowing whether the boy was going to live or die, I realised I had been given an opportunity to 'give back'. A few years earlier, my son had been rescued from just such a road accident a few miles from that very spot, and I felt truly honoured to have been given this opportunity to perform a service in gratitude for all that was done for my son at the time by the Thai people.

The next day we left the islands for Northern Thailand, to learn something of the tribal culture which still remains in the foothills there. Temperatures were hovering in the 40's with high humidity and we began to seek air conditioning wherever we went. Due to the language barrier, I was also beginning to feel a little isolated. We hadn't found any good books or music, and our thoughts were straying toward England's green and pleasant land, the rolling hills of Dorset, and hugs from our loved ones.

## BUDDHIST TEMPLES

We travelled to the city of Chiang Mai which is dominated by Thailand's most sacred site, the mountain-top temple of Wat Phrathat Doi Suthep. The temple complex itself is surrounded by bells of all sizes, many of which were almost as big as me. We were encouraged to ring them - for cleansing and for good luck. Before entering the central, shining, 'golden' temple (it is actually clad in copper), we duly removed our shoes and were greeted by the monk who presides over the temple. He threw water over us before chanting prayers as we knelt on the carpeted floor of the temple beneath countless images of Buddha. I felt truly honoured to receive such a blessing in this sacred place.

The next day we went to a meditation class run by a young monk in a temple in the city, and were lucky enough to find ourselves the only two students! We enjoyed instruction in:

- 'Insight' meditation, which is practiced while walking

- 'Concentration' meditation, which can be practiced amidst chaos by focusing on something still, like a glass

of water, and holding this concentration so that anything
happening around you has no effect

- Non-attachment Buddhist philosophy:
  ◊ IMPERMANENCE - that nothing in this life or world
  is permanent and everything is constantly changing.
  ◊ SUFFERING - is attachment, anger and ignorance but
  by controlling the mind we can bring an end to suffering
  ◊ NON SELF - that our body is borrowed from the earth
  and will be returned to the earth when we die

## TAO GARDEN HEALTH RESORT

One of the highlights of our visit to Thailand was a visit to Tao
Garden, a world renowned award-winning health resort and
spa, where a Master of Tao Philosophy has a Training School
and which attracts people from across the globe. We had
arranged the visit on the spur of the moment and immediately
felt at home. Of course we were destined to go there, although
we did not know it at the time.

Our accommodation consisted of a small studio flat with a
desk area, a sink, a fridge and a good bathroom. It was light and
airy, surrounded by trees and plants and close to the morning
Chi Kung area and the swimming pool, yet not far from the
open-air restaurant and offices. The theme of the spa was YING
YANG and there were many circular buildings and areas
designated to spirituality within the garden, as well as several
small lakes and ponds and a river running through it. The
wildlife was plentiful, with geckos of all sizes, butterflies,
monkeys calling in the distance, and many, many birds amongst
the magnificent trees and flowers.

## MASSAGE

Here I received several very special healing Chi Nei Tsang

treatments - internal organ 'Chi' massage above the navel and surrounding abdominal area where stress, tension and negative emotions accumulate and congest. I also benefitted from several Karzai Nei Tsang treatments where the practitioner employs sensitive but deep pressure and small circular massage movements to dissolve the sedimentation in the circulatory system, release the toxicity in the organs, and assist the student in letting go of any past emotional blockages held in those areas.

Thailand was definitely a period of clearing out more old patterns from within the body, mind and spirit. What with the cleanse and detox on Koh Samui island, followed by two weeks of inner massage work, I was a sucker for punishment!

## CHI KUNG (Qigong)

We joined both teachers and students for morning and evening Chi Kung sessions. The Senior Instructor, Andrew Fretwell, was an ex rock star from England, whose life had been completely turned around through Taoist work, and whom we subsequently hosted back in Dorset to introduce his work to my clients and to further develop our own understanding. The Chi Kung Form which Andrew taught us has been a highly beneficial practice both for me and my clients, working as it does on the entire energy system of the body, promoting good health for both body and mind, honouring all the directions.

## HEALING LOVE

We also signed up for the 'Healing Love' course for couples which offered Taoist and Tantra techniques to reinforce the bond between men and women so that their best human qualities can shine forth; with ritual steps for integration, letting go and forgiveness, as it is difficult to love when we are resentful. Resentment grows in the mind, eating away at the liver's life force. Resentment scorns love. It is said that only death or forgiveness transforms resentment. "For love to deepen, the heart must open even more."

## Tao and Tantra

One of the simple steps we learned involved creating sacred space in our relationship, finding time to practice an exercise of sitting opposite each other on the floor and looking into one another's eyes and synchronizing our breathing - one inhaling while the other exhales - causing orgasmic energy to spread throughout the body. The intention of these practices is for each partner to honour the other and therefore deepen love. We were encouraged to set aside specific times to develop our practice together. Sexual energy is deeply honoured, as it is considered to be the same as life force and is used to increase health and longevity. They promote practices which heighten awareness of how we can retain this life force, in order to have good health and to live longer. In the West we only seem to be aware that the act of love is pleasurable, reduces stress hormones and increases serotonin!

## The Inner Smile

This work included learning the 'Inner Smile' Meditation in which we smile inwardly to each of the major organs of our body, activating the energy of loving-kindness, and waking up the Five Element network which governs our organs and emotions. When any of these elements in our body or in our environment are balanced, we experience health and prosperity. When they're out of balance we can experience dis-ease of one sort or another.

## Six Healing Sounds for Health

We also learnt a breathing meditation which would enable us to transform our "shit into honey", as our teachers delighted in telling us. First you breathe air in through the nose and then let it out slowly through the mouth. One way of drawing breath in, and six ways of expelling breath out, using the Chinese syllables: To expel heat (chway); to expel cold (hoo); to relieve tension (shee); to release anger (her); to display malaise (hsü); and to regain equilibrium (sss). Each of these six vibrations has a psychic influence on a corresponding organ, promoting the expulsion of impurities and gathering fresh energy into each system. The version I teach my clients is a slightly European version connected to each of the main organs: lung (ssss); kidney (choo); liver (shhhh); heart (hawww); spleen (whoo); and triple warmer (heee).

As a grand finale to our visit, Norm and I, as 'elders' in the camp, were invited to take part in a Water Ceremony (more ceremony) - the Songkran New Year celebrations, during which the young women all dress in traditional costume and perform dances. Forty people lined up to pour water over our hands to bless us and wish us a happy new year, their tradition being to honour the elders of the family / village for their wisdom and help. People spent the whole day pouring water over one another at home, in the streets, everywhere you went. It was great fun and had a spiritual purpose too - water being the symbol of purification. Amidst much hilarity, a good time was had by all. I am beginning to think that that would be a great ceremony to introduce in our country, just as I hold 'Croning and Crowning' ceremonies to celebrate the wise older woman. I crown women with a garland of flowers to celebrate and honour who they are and where they have come to in their lives. Our older generation is not honoured enough.

**EGYPT**

Here we moved into a sense of humility. Egypt is a deeply spiritual country, but it also manifests a type of earthly, crazy chaos particularly evident in their driving habits. Motorists cross traffic lanes helter-skelter, incessantly hooting horns and narrowly escaping a crash every few seconds.

For years I had longed to visit the great pyramids of Giza, one of the great energy points on earth. There are as many theories about the true purpose of the pyramids as there are about who built them and how they were built. When I actually gazed up at these giant structures, I was even more mystified as to how the gigantic stone cubes found their way into their positions, creating such symmetry and surviving for so long. Our guide told us that most of the stones weigh 2.5 tons, while some weigh as much as 50 tons. There are 2.3 million blocks in total which together weigh 6 million tons - truly astonishing.

As our guide was shepherding us toward the middle of the three pyramids and politely asking if we wanted to venture inside, I explained that I was here to fulfil my long-held dream to enter the Great Pyramid. He shook his head explaining that there were only one hundred and fifty tickets issued and that we would be too late. Nevertheless, he hurried us along to the booking office where we were able to purchase the last two tickets! This was the beginning of a morning of divine synchronicity.

As we approached the Great Pyramid, our guide suddenly announced that he would meet us at the exit and hurried away leaving us to our own devices, with no clue as to what might happen next. We climbed the steps to the entrance where we met three Egyptian gentlemen, one of whom spoke a smattering of English. He asked us how long we would want to pray once we entered the Kings burial chamber. "Fifteen minutes" I replied. He then consulted with his colleagues before taking my hand and guiding me into the pyramid with Norm following behind. I assumed this was common practice, and only discovered later that it was most unusual. I very quickly realised why this gentleman was holding my hand as we began to climb steep wooden ladders with a single handrail at a forty-five degree angle up a low dark tunnel, so that our bodies were almost bent double as there was no headroom. We were like scarab beetles scrabbling up this tunnel. We climbed and climbed up more than seventy-five steps. There was a moment when we could have chosen to go a different route to the 'Queen's Burial Tomb', a route which looked even more terrifying. The second steeper stairway led to the King's Chamber, which is situated at the central point within the pyramid. If we had slipped, I think we might have met our doom. At last we reached the summit. The whole experience so removed from how I had imagined it would be - descending gently into a brightly painted, illuminated tomb - that my bravado at having overcome my claustrophobia in the caves of New Zealand was being sorely tested!

We paused at the entrance to the tomb for a moment to allow a couple to leave who were speaking French and unaccompanied by a guide. In the faint light emanating from the King's chamber, we could make out two men talking to each other, and the actual tomb which stood about three feet off the floor. Our guide then exhorted us not to speak within the chamber, emphasising that within that space there must be total silence or he would be in trouble. To say I was disappointed is an understatement. In one of the most powerful energy centres of the world, having taken our life in our hands to get here, I was not to be allowed to sing aloud. How come the other people were chattering and how come they didn't have a guide? No matter, I thought, I would simply kneel, as in any sacred space, close my eyes and meditate, which is what I did.

As soon as the two men left, the guide took us both by the hand and led us into the central point of the chamber. He lifted our hands above our heads - I imagined that we were reaching toward the apex of the pyramid; he then appeared to begin energy work by putting his hands on each of our chests in turn. We held this position for a few minutes and I think he uttered a prayer before hugging us both. He then led us towards the sarcophagus and gestured for me to climb in and lie down. While I felt honoured, I also felt a little fearful. After a little while I climbed out and Norman climbed in. The guide led me back into the centre of the chamber, blessed me and hugged me, weeping and eventually explaining his weeping as being "for the Mother". I had no idea what he meant by this statement. He then repeated the ritual for Norm and wished us both well before leading us back down the tortuous ladders.

As we left the pyramid, we finally realised that none of the other entrants had been accompanied and that we had been privileged to experience a private energetic session in the King's chamber. Ungrounded and overwhelmed by the power of the energy we had experienced – it was as if I had received a massive bolt of lightning - I had to walk and move very carefully for fear of falling over, eventually collapsing into bed in our hotel room and falling into a deep sleep. I later discovered that one theory pertaining to that chamber is that it was used as a sacred initiation centre and I realised that we had indeed been given an 'Initiation'. Apparently, in ancient times, students who had first undergone long years of preparation, meditation and metaphysical instruction in an esoteric school, were placed in the granite coffer of the main chamber and left alone throughout an entire night. The coffer was the focal point of the energies gathered, concentrated, aimed and directed at the main chamber by virtue of the precise mathematical location, alignment and construction of the pyramid, conducive to the awakening, stimulation and acceleration of spiritual consciousness in the suitably prepared adept. In my recent reading of a book by Claire Heartsong called "Anna, Grandmother of Jesus", she speaks of how Jesus himself was taken into this very chamber and placed in the sarcophagus. She describes how it was designed to help initiates awaken to the remembrance of their true identity.

The bolt of lightning I felt was clearly part of the process of my own limited identity dying, in order to make way for a new identity. There have been various turning points in my life such as this, where I felt something change in my body, but this was one of the biggest. This great alignment which occurs when the universal power assists us in enlarging our sense of caring for others' wellbeing, and our ability to be more compassionately present in all of our relationships.

What an experience it had been. Nothing planned, no verbal communication; a lesson in offering oneself into the possibility; following; going with the flow of whatever; letting go of any form of control and the fear that comes with that; and so allowing the magic to occur.

Our Egyptian adventures continued as we cruised down the Nile to Luxor and Aswan, taking in the extraordinary sites of ancient and present day Egypt. We caught our sleeper back to Cairo with great reluctance. After that it was on to Vienna.

## AUSTRIA

Arriving in Vienna we spotted a statue of Joseph Haydn outside a very ordinary church and immediately felt drawn to go inside. An organist was playing a Bach prelude. Within a minute or two, tears were rolling down my cheeks and I could feel Norm's emotions rising beside me too. It was a sound so evocative of Europe, to which we had returned after seven months. It felt like a true homecoming and such a contrast to the sounds of the cities of Egypt. We had come from chaos to order and precision in this architecturally magnificent city.

Our stomachs calling, we looked for somewhere to eat, quite soon falling upon Café Mozart, renowned for its wiener schnitzel which was indeed delicious.

We had pre-booked the tickets for the Vienna State Opera House as it had been a dream of Norm's for years. We were to see a modern production of Die Zauberflote - The Magic Flute. It was with slight trepidation but also with a feeling of some amusement that we arrived at the Opera House and moved up the grand staircase rubbing elbows with men and women in evening attire, dressed in our travel togs. The beauty of it was that no-one turned a hair although I think if we had been at Covent Garden we might have received a few strange looks.

Norm considers Opera to be the ultimate art form, a spectacle that combines music, singing, dance and sometimes spoken word and we were not disappointed by the spectacle, in fact we felt exhilarated by the performance on all levels.

The next day we visited the Musikverein, the 'Golden Hall' which is home to The Vienna Philharmonic, one of the world's greatest orchestras, and from where the BBC TV New Year's Day concert is transmitted annually. There was such a sense of presence in that gold painted room but the only tickets available were for a performance of the Vienna Boys' Choir in the 'Brahms Salle'. We duly purchased them, and what a treat it was to hear those young boys deliver the songs of their culture with such enthusiasm, sense of fun, and yet with perfect precision.

Vienna is a cultural centre renowned for its architecture and music, the birthplace of Schubert and Johann Strauss, and the home of Beethoven, Mozart, Brahms, Mahler and many of the world's great conductors. We felt awed and inspired in the presence of such majesty. Norm was so taken with it all he was dreaming of moving into Mahler's old flat, now a coffee bar!

## HOME

We landed at Heathrow after travelling for almost seven months. My children were there to greet us. How beautiful it was to be received back into Great Britain with their love and excitement. I had waited many weeks for that day. Homecoming is different for us all. It depends largely on where home is for each of us and where our roots are. I understand that spiritually we reach home when we die, or when we become fully enlightened. However, when we find home within ourselves we feel centred, rooted and are not rocked off balance by any outside circumstances - of which there had been many on our pilgrimage.

Although I have only described a few highlights of our journey, I hope I have demonstrated the power of pilgrimage, how prayers can be answered, how if we surrender and trust in the process, incredible beauty and love can appear. It is a joyous and remarkable way of getting to know oneself.

Chapter Twelve

# RELEASING THE OLD TO RECEIVE THE NEW

*May all that is unforgiven in you*
*Be released.*
*May your fears yield*
*Their deepest tranquilities.*
*May all that is unlived in you*
*Blossom into a future graced with love.*

John O'Donohue

MY FATHER WAS ninety-six when we set off on our world pilgrimage and seemed curiously unhappy to see us go. I remember him expressing a lack of understanding of why people feel the need to leave England - the green and pleasant land! I realise now that he had been ready to die. Thankfully, he waited for our return before he began his process towards death. I was so privileged to be his witness and loyal friend over a period of six months as he gradually and consciously withdrew from life. I was able to sit with him, often in silence. Simply being present with one another in the presence of LOVE was healing for both of us. Towards the end my mother was also able to join us. When the time came, my brother and I arranged a beautiful cremation and memorial service in his local church full of music and words from people whose hearts had been touched by this wise, gentle owl of a man who loved music, canal and river cruising, and sport.

I was catapulted into a level of grief I had not experienced before and it turned my life upside down. My loss was enormous. I had loved my father dearly and life did not seem to make sense without him. There is so much energy tied up in our relationships with our parents, which can be the most precious of relationships and at the same time the most complicated. Mine had been somewhat tangled. My father had been a deeply spiritual, loving being, gentle, honourable, humorous, generous and light hearted. He was known as a man of great integrity to all in the family and everyone I knew that met him felt his warm, loyal and deeply loving presence. There was darkness within him too; a shadow which I imagine was some kind of depression. He was often very quiet.

I always felt love and honour for my father even when I discovered the truth of our story. He was a man of such integrity.

It was in my late fifties, that my thirst to complete a missing part of my family jigsaw led me to seek out a five-day residential course for 'survivors' of trauma. I felt that the psychotherapist running the week long course might be able to assist me through this journey because the course had a particular way of looking at trauma in conjunction with the function of the limbic brain - sometimes known as the emotional brain. Whenever we perceive a threat a neurochemical change occurs in the limbic system directly affecting the adrenal glands - the well-known 'fight or flight' response to fear. The limbic brain stores these fear-based experiences and their associated emotions and because the limbic brain controls the autonomic nervous system, we can connect with the memories stored in the body. Tapping into those memories can give a much fuller picture during the course of a particular event.

After completing an in depth questionnaire into the history of our blood-family, and entering into deep discussions around the information I supplied, it began to dawn on me that my relationship with my father had been that of a classic 'princess'. He had not only put me on a pedestal, but had made inappropriate approaches which were not to be spoken of to anyone, and were to be 'our secret'. This insight triggered long buried memories from when I was seven. As children, the classic response to traumas is to deny them because they feel so immense. Classically, I had denied my own situation and while it was painful to uncover the truth, I knew it was the only way to be free of this deeply significant and disturbing chapter of my life.

The week was spent in group carrying out exercises to access the memories stored in our bodies. Everyone had experienced trauma of some kind. After the course, I continued to journey with this work for some six months before I could finally release the pain which my body had been carrying. A great weight finally lifted and I found myself speaking with a new voice. A voice that was less self-critical and less critical of others too. Unsurprisingly, my relationship with my husband improved as a direct result of this work. He was an enormous help to me during the whole process, offering much needed masculine support and nurture. I began to move into a place of deep forgiveness and understanding of how and why it had happened.

Now I rest in the knowledge that all is well and that the experience had been an important part of my life path, enabling me to assist others who have had similar experiences. I have long processed it all, to such an extent that I am asking my father for help as I write. He is a great friend and ally now, although and because he is on the other side.

At the time of losing my father I had a very intense response to his loss. I was not able to be of help to my mother or brother. I even began to shut the door on Norman, my soul mate and great love. I did not feel that anyone could understand what I was going through. I needed to be alone, and took a six-month sabbatical from everyone and everything. It was another turning point in my life. It was a painful time, and yet I felt that my heart was opening to something new and revealing. While endings are painful and awkward, once the heart assimilates that that particular stage of a relationship has run its course - has come to an end on the surface of our time - its presence, meaning and effect continues to be held and integrated in the eternal - leaving a feeling of wholeness and authenticity.

I cried and sang incessantly using all of my practices to support me in the process. When our defences collapse through shock and grief, a door opens to receive love and opportunities, so that grieving can also be a time of great healing, particularly of our hearts. The actual process of letting go allows us to receive.

We can practice bringing love towards us by just allowing sound from the highest source to come through us by singing our sound without words, just by taking a breath and sounding out:

- from the heavens through the crown of the head down to the heart
- from the earth through the feet and up to the heart
- surrendering and allowing this sound to come from the highest source fills us up with LOVE

This filling up with LOVE, and embodying and grounding that LOVE, took me back to that inner part of myself which is whole. When I realised I could connect with that part so simply and easily, and feel and know that LOVE, it shifted me into new ways of being and it encouraged me to practice.

Practice seems to be the key. Regular practice enables us to reacquaint ourselves with our wholeness. When I feel whole it is easier to make decisions about life and to love both myself and others around me. So that while I was going through the heart breaking process of letting go of my father, living in a rented apartment in a Wiltshire market town, I found myself not only newly allied to a Buddhist community, who were a great source of comfort to me, but also embarked on setting up a professional healing practice. My ability to carry on amidst the turmoil was certainly related to this Presence of being.

Not long after that, my beautiful daughter gave birth to her firstborn.

## RECEIVING THE NEW

Tallulah Rose lit up my life, as all four of our grandchildren and step-grandchildren have done, yet her arrival was particularly poignant as it shone such a bright light on the darkness that had shrouded my father's departure. My experience has been that Life/LOVE/God brings us amazing gifts to help us in our hour of need.

When I held her for the first time I remembered the words of a friend - "when grandchildren come into your life you fall in love all over again" - which is exactly how I felt. It was the beginning of a new generation in our family. I felt proud of my daughter and her partner, Lee. My son came to visit shortly after the birth and was equally besotted with this new soul in our lives and we celebrated together. I was also honoured to be asked to facilitate Tallulah's Naming Ceremony – well before my training as a Minister – but between us we managed it well! Because there hadn't been a marriage at that stage, it was the first time both families had come together, so it had the flavor and excitement of a wedding.

When this little angel graced us with her presence, she heralded a new cycle and a new purpose in our lives. Not that 'angel' would be the first word which comes into our thoughts about Tallulah these days! She has a strong voice and demands to be heard. She is a leader by nature with a depth of compassion and care for others. I particularly honour this in Tallulah as it took me sixty years and a lot of hard work to come to that place of leadership!

At Naming Ceremonies nowadays, I remind parents that we are not only honoring the child but also our Creator/God/LOVE, whatever term you want to use, and encourage them to see the spirit and beauty which they see in the child reflected in themselves. Over the years my step-grandsons Nathaniel and Nicholas and my granddaughters Tallulah and Liliana have played, sung, danced, painted, walked and swum with me; reminding me what childhood is all about and reassuring the child and divine spirit within me. Their presence in my life has been and still remains an ongoing source of healing for me.

After my father passed away, my mother who was in her late eighties, had frequent bouts of bronchitis and I suggested that she came to live near me in Wiltshire so that I could assist in her day-to-day care. She agreed, on the basis that "you don't put me in a home". We moved her into a single storey apartment which was part of a converted stable block, surrounded by beautiful gardens, just a ten-minute drive from my house. She settled in well, and we introduced her to a circle of people who played bridge, a game she enjoyed, and we spent many days and hours together talking happily about daily life or the weather or politics, which had always interested her. I so wanted to speak with her about life and love, but most of her generation - who had lived through the second world war - developed stiff upper lips and never discussed anything 'difficult'. Although I was spending more time with her than I had ever done in my life, it just wasn't possible to have what I call a 'real' conversation - one where you can get into thoughts and feelings about anything personal.

There was, however, to be a little miracle, to come in this regard.

Six years on, as I prepare this book for publication, I am also preparing myself for my own mother's ending, for it does not feel far off. She is ninety-five and beginning to fade. She has given us all a few rehearsals; her carers call her the "cat with nine lives". She has vascular dementia. The arteries of the brain are narrowing and there seem to be major changes going on as a result. She no longer worries like she did, because she is neither remembering the past, nor seeing the future. Through this process, she seems to be softening and our love is gaining new strength. She is very much loved by both my brother and me. We both hold her in deep empathy and compassion now. The hours spent sitting in her room at her bedside have been a practice for me, almost always a pleasure. The depth of love and compassion I feel for her is beyond words. During one of those days I decided to speak of my relationship with my father, something I had wanted to do for so long. It felt the right time and indeed it was. Unlike all the years I have tried to speak with her, this time there was absolutely no resistance. She listened intently and was surprised to hear the story. She expressed her deep sorrow and then proceeded to share that she too had had an experience with her own father making unwanted advances towards her. We united utterly and completely and something huge fell away from me in the process and almost certainly from her. It was the first time in my sixty-six years that I felt I was sitting in my truth with my mother, and her with me. How precious this has been for us both. A moment of everlasting magic – another layer of the mask fell away that day.

## HONOURING THE MOTHER

*We share the truth of who we are*
*I am the fruit of her womb*
*She gave me life*
*We are not separate.*
*She is a part of me and I her.*
*Her soul alights with mine*
*As the autumn mists cross the fields*
*The spiders' webs weave their magic*
*On the branches of the oak.*
*The rich red holly berries*
*Are the blood of our being*
*Bearing fruits at this time*
*To signify the fire, the fire of her being...*
*Our Great Mother...*
*What great joy there is in her as in all mothers*
*As fragile as the holly berry*
*Its juice...her blood running thru' her body.*
*Take me home, she speaks*
*Take me home...home is where the fire burns*
*In the grate, keeping the home fire burning*
*So that life is not extinguished*
*The flame is alive in my heart - and in hers*
*They momentarily collide and meet*
*Singing the tune of the one heart,*
*The one sound, the one wild, wonderful*
*Voice of the Great Mother. Ohm.*

*Written at my mother's bedside towards the end of her life*

                                        *Hilary Eliza Franklin*

## RESOURCES

The Survivors Trust
www.thesurvivorstrust.org

Chapter Thirteen

# CHARTRES PILGRIMAGE

*"Every day is a journey and the journey itself is home."*

Matsuo Basho

LOOKING BACK IN my sixtieth year, it was almost unbelievable to think that there had been a time when I had been hobbling around on two sticks. Nonetheless, I knew that my left hip now needing replacing and so willingly underwent that operation. Then to celebrate my sixtieth birthday, I planned a three stage pilgrimage to include the wells of Wales (and for those that don't know, wells are usually sacred sites representing the Sacred Feminine); the cathedral at Chartres in France; and the Celtic isles of Scotland. Two women friends, one of whom shared an interest in the two Christian Mary's, Mother Mary and Mary Magdalene - were to join me for the second stage to Our Lady of Chartres Cathedral, which is where I experienced one of the most magical happenings of my life.

The Cathedral is built on an earth 'power point' where electro-magnetic forces come to the surface, and is crossed by the feminine energy ley line which Mary Magdalene is reputed to have travelled, reaching 900 miles from the south of France, through Chartres, Avebury, Stonehenge, Rosslyn Chapel, to Holyrood in Scotland. The orientation of the building is not typical of most Christian churches. It sits on an axis which allows the midsummer sunrise to pour through the glorious Rose Window into the centre of the Labyrinth - exactly as it does through the stones of Stonehenge.

Gordon Strachan in his book 'Sacred Space, Sacred Geometry' explains that the unique combination of earth energies, the marriage of Christian and Islamic architecture, coupled with the mysticism and skills of the medieval geometers and craftsmen, came together to fashion a spectacularly powerful place of inspiration and spiritual transformation. Strachan's diagram demonstrates how the energy centres of the cathedral match those of the human body, which is particularly fascinating because the most frequented locations in the building coincide with the Heart at the Crossing, where nave, transept and chancel meet, and the Sacral Chakra at the Labyrinth.

The Labyrinth combines flower images and a path which unites the masculine and feminine traditions - pilgrims tread the pathway with Christ yet their journey is also held and sustained by Mary his mother, represented by the mystic petalled Rose at the centre of the Labyrinth and echoed by the Rose window above. In this crucible, where masculine and feminine are in balance and where love moves, transformation and healing can take place. The one path design represents a journey in which there are no decisions to be made - as when we surrender to walking a spiritual path in life - our only decision is to choose Spirit/God and surrender to divine guidance. It is non-denominational and anyone longing to re-connect to the divine may find peace and a sense of divine presence in this open-eyed meditation. After reflecting in the centre, the walker reverses direction, coming back into the mundane world from a centered and enlightened mind. It is humbling to think that pilgrims have walked this circular path for almost eight hundred years.

My friends and I moved into the labyrinth barefoot. Chrissie led the way, followed by me and then Patsy. I was carrying a large clear quartz crystal, the altar centrepiece of our 'Mary' group. As I entered, I asked for Divine Guidance as to what step I should take next in fulfilling my life's purpose. We walked slowly, intently and ceremoniously. As we reached the different loops of the Labyrinth, of which there are eleven full circuits and many more turns with the loops, we paused, feeling the change and shift in energy. Each twist and turn felt like a metaphor for life - almost reaching the heart and the next minute moving away, out again and then back again. I was aware of a connection with the Great Mother, with Mary the Christian Mother, and with all women. I was also conscious of a single man moving ahead of us at exactly the same slow pace - as if balancing our feminine presence with the masculine.

Nearing the centre, I experienced a rush of energy and deep emotion and tears of joy sprang into my eyes. It was bliss. Then, as I placed the quartz crystal in the very centre of the Rose, I felt overwhelmed with LOVE, a feeling of coming home to GOD. Tears poured out of me as I knelt and touched my head and hands to the floor, giving thanks for being present in this heavenly sacred space, adding a prayer for the healing of the feminine in us all, both men and women. When I raised myself up at last, I connected eye-to-eye with my friends, seeing the joy and compassion written on their faces. We gently moved into each of the six Rose petals. A word sprung to my mind as I entered each one: faith, hope, harmony, love, compassion and forgiveness. I could have stayed there forever, but aware that other pilgrims were making their way toward us; we had to return along the path. Hesitant at first, I gradually found myself walking with a sense of ease, freedom, lightness, joy and with a spring in my step. It was a momentous experience, one which continues to live through me.

We made our way down into the crypt, which was lined with medieval frescoes and filled with small chapels and exquisite stain-glassed windows. We found the well dedicated to 'Our Lady under the Earth', where an effigy of a black Madonna represents both the Earth Mother and the Mother of Jesus combined. We also managed to get ourselves locked in, which for some reason we found extremely funny. Thankfully we managed to retrace our steps and find a way out.

The answer to my request for guidance began to unfold very quickly. I found myself talking to my friends about the possibility of training to be a minister - to become 'the priestess'. I believed my prayer was being answered because as I spoke about this notion I recognized an inner exhilaration and anticipation - a personal sign that an idea is fully aligned with my soul, and as soon as I returned home I began to research ministerial training.

There is a legend about Chartres that when Europe was immersed in the Crusades, the great families sent their sons off to fight in those holy wars while the common people sent their sons to build the cathedral. I love this story because it demonstrates that a community working in harmony can create great things. It also reminds us that we can choose positive action over disharmony; creation is the natural opposite of destruction. If we ever feel taken over by anger or aggression, performing a creative action such as writing a song or poem, painting, gardening, cooking or playing with children, shifts our perspective and consciousness.

---

**RESOURCES**

'Sacred Space, Sacred Geometry' *by Gordon Strachan*
'The Two Mary's: The Hidden History of the
Mother and Wife of Jesus'
*by Sylvia Brown*

---

# PART THREE

Chapter Fourteen

# MINISTRY

*"God receives us just as we are. But we don't receive ourselves in the same way. We don't love ourselves as we are. Our deepest work is not so much to improve ourselves as to realize ourselves, to see ourselves clearly and dearly."*

Jason Shulman

MY JOURNEY THROUGH the Labyrinth in Chartres was the inspiration that led me to enter into Ministry with the One Spirit Interfaith Foundation. It had been over fifteen years since I realised that I could no longer take part fully in church services and could only be a witness to them. As a seeker and a searcher by nature, the more dogmatic traditions of the Church of England had not always captivated my imagination and yet I loved their ritual and ceremony. I also did not resonate with their understanding of sin, and the ensuing guilt and shame on which the Christian faith is based. I had begun to believe that I could forgive myself for what I would have considered to be sins in the past; that I could forgive others who I have felt had wronged me and that the things that go wrong in life are merely lessons to be learned, gifts to help us evolve, like the illness that had set me on the path that had led me right to this moment.

A telephone interview was set up, and I was accepted on the training to become an Interfaith Minister and Spiritual Counsellor beginning in October 2010 at the London home of the Sufis, at Colet House in Hammersmith. It was a stretch financially as it involved both travel and accommodation costs, but I knew it was meant to be.

Our group of trainees consisted of thirty-nine men and women from Scotland, Ireland and England. Our ages ranged from thirty-five to seventy-two representing many different cultures and creeds - a diversity that brought great richness to our studies and to our personal experiences throughout the training.

We were invited to introduce ourselves by speaking or singing, and of course I chose the latter...no words, just the sounds from my heart. Our first exercise in pairs was to reflect to one another "Why are you here and what is your heart's longing?" I replied that I was here because my soul was compelling me to be here (a voice deep inside me which I can't explain but know is right and cannot help following) and that I wanted to develop myself further as a conduit, a human vessel through which others could connect to their own spirit.

The first year's curriculum involved researching the six major faith paths and traditions. We would be visiting houses of worship, speaking to people practising those faiths, and then exploring our own relationship with each faith through various practices including: reflecting on our attractions; intolerances; ways to inner and outer peace; how the different traditions affected our world view; and our way of being in relationship with our self and others. During the year we were to study the scriptures of the various religions, in addition to reading Huston Smith's 'World Religions' and Mathew Fox's 'One River, Many Wells' plus many others from a huge list. Most importantly, we were to practice a daily ritual from each faith for a month.

They were looking for depth of experience, research and authentic heart-felt reflection and wanted quality, not quantity in our assignments. Each involved the same four questions:

- What has attracted you within this faith path, and how can you apply this within your own journey?

- What has challenged you within this faith path and what can you do, inwardly and outwardly, to address this challenge within yourself?

- What would you say is the essence of this path - as a student of the Interfaith Seminary?

- Having entered into this journey what has shifted in terms of your worldview?

Placed in study groups consisting of six students, it was our responsibility to arrange a monthly meeting with each other for half a day to create a space for us to integrate our studies and experiences of the training. It would provide a forum through which to deepen our spiritual enquiry, to support and learn from each other through our diversity. A peer mentor, who had completed her training the previous year, was also assigned to each group to support us by attending many of the study group meetings, as well as facilitating monthly individual hour-long sessions on Skype.

## THE DIFFERENT FAITH PATHS
Whilst visiting the six major religions (Buddhism, Hinduism, Judaism, Christianity, Islam and The Earth Traditions), we were invited to allow our world view to expand by looking at how we see ourselves in relation to the Divine, to one another and

to the Earth. To look at how we see God, how that affects our life and how we choose to be as a result. Our tutors Rev. Nicola Coombe (Head of the Seminary) and Rev. Jackie Amos Wilkinson explained that the training was an opportunity to see the depth of our own faith, to find a pathway that suited us as individuals, to see how that might be enhanced, expanded and modified, and to discover our own essential nature through connection with God.

## HINDUISM

The essence of this path is somehow in line with the essence of the Interfaith Seminary in that Truth, or God, is one, that our real nature is divine and that it is perfectly acceptable for there to be innumerable spiritual pathways, all leading to this realization of our own divinity and oneness with God. I was told by the Hindu priest I spoke to that he considers Hinduism to be not so much a religion as "a way of life". Its essence, as I see it, is that of personal transformation through various ancient practices which have been proven to offer a path to freeing ourselves of human suffering – actualising our divine self through spiritual discipline.

Hinduism shows us the importance of discipline in our spiritual practices. There are four main systems within Hinduism as a pathway to God, so there are choices for different personality types: through knowledge; work; psychophysical exercise and the body; and through LOVE - all ways to the same truth. Yoga is a system for recognising earthly life for what it is, and identifying with our eternal being at the same time. The word Yoga means 'to yoke the soul back to God', which is the ultimate aim of the Hindu tradition and is so in keeping with the ethics of Interfaith. In the word AUM, the most sacred of sounds, the A stands for God the Creator - Brahma; the U for God the Preserver of Souls - Vishnu; and M for God the Destroyer of Illusion - Shiva.

## THE EARTH TRADITIONS

Our speaker took us on a meditation Journey into the underworld, through a process of drumming known as Journeying. Journeying is a profound practice which I use regularly. I am drawn to the rhythm and sound of the drum, and I work with it for myself and for others to travel into the depths of the underworld and up to the heights of the world above the heavens, to meet with our ancestors and other spiritual beings. The ancient sound of the drum and other sounds that I work with as a sound healer are tools for accessing our souls. Our homework for the Interfaith training was to both be outside in nature and to chant as much as possible.

The main earth traditions include Paganism, Wicca and Shamanism and it is Shamanism that seems to draw me. I had already worked with two shamanic teachers and taken part in two major rituals which created powerful changes in my life which enabled me to walk a more independent and self-fulfilling path as a result. Both experiences took place in the inhospitable landscape of the Mexican desert.

One ritual involved picking and eating the sacred peyote plant for hallucinatory wisdom prior to a pilgrimage through the desert. This pilgrimage seemed beyond my own physical ability, but during the walk my father came into my conscious-ness with words of encouragement which was a blessing indeed and I overcame all the obstacles and ended up becoming 'the leader' with a new inner and outer strength.

The other involved a live burial, in which I dug my own grave in the desert, laid in it with a witness and friend to cover me completely in the earth, except for my face of course, whilst I was encouraged by the Shaman to relate my complete life story, however long it would take, to the witness and friend. I lay in the grave, for a period of 3 hours without being able to move other than to breathe. It is a ritual to enable you to free yourself from any attachment to your personal story and an opportunity to uncover any secrets. There was something very funny about my witness and friend, in that she was Mexican and hardly spoke a word of English, so understood nothing I said, which seemed perfect for me.

Through its map, the Medicine Wheel, Shamanism has taught me the connection between the points of the compass, without and within, by working with the 'Four Directions' and 'Six Directions' to create sacred space. It has been particularly useful to me when I am offering a ritualistic or ceremonial space in my work.

The essence of the Shamanic path is 'connection with spirit in its many forms', particularly in the form of animals and all plants and things earthbound. The Shaman works with the Medicine wheel as a springboard of power, to enable us to link to divine energies and the universe.

A deep sense of my own soul arises out of my work with the Shamanic tradition; through the power of the awareness of the spirit of animal life, the spirit of plant life, and the spirit of a world beneath the earth, in addition to the power of the moon, the sun, the stars, other planets and a world above us. This awareness was not shown to me in my original Christian upbringing, and I have found hidden depths in how to live my life in harmony with all these aspects of life which surround us. It has given me a greater knowledge and wisdom of connecting to the inner and the outer God. I see myself as being part of all that surrounds me, and so I honour myself in the same way as I honour the magnificence of the flowers, trees, animals, oceans, rivers, mountains and sky. My faith path has to include the powerful recognition that we are all interconnected, and that no one species is any more powerful than the other. This faith path opens me to an ancient wisdom about living, growing and healing.

## JUDAISM

I visited a beautiful synagogue in Birmingham with my Jewish friend. It was a wonderful day and there was much that drew me toward this path. Firstly, the fact that their spiritual practice ran through their everyday life, particularly within the family home. I loved their weekly family ritual on a Friday evening when they light candles and declare the following twenty-four hours as Shabbat – a sacred day in which ALL the family takes part. I liked the way eating, drinking and fasting is part of their spiritual practice. I liked their celebration of all the festivals and the way in which they acknowledge the essence of each cycle of the year - not unlike the Earth traditions.

The essence of this path I believe to be based upon strong family units which can at times be exclusive in its practices, particularly in their Orthodox Church. A Jew believes that God is outside himself, that God and nature are distinct, and that all that God created is there to be valued as a process of salvation. Therefore, Jews appreciate the physical world, possessions and sex. They do not believe in original sin. It is essential for them to study and believe in the Torah and the story of Abraham, which does not feel in keeping with the essence of Interfaith. Although Liberal Judaism is much more open, as I experienced when I visited the Liberal synagogue in Birmingham, it still feels very prescriptive. Yet, as a people, I experienced them as very welcoming, friendly and open hearted – they welcomed me to a study group meeting, as well as a service. However, the services are all words coming from the Siddur Lev Chadash either spoken or chanted. Finally, I felt the essence of the path to be limiting.

## WORK PLACEMENT

At this point in the training, we were asked to arrange a work placement for ourselves. We were to choose one which would test us to the edge, and one which was within our comfort zone, both to be completed by the end of the training. I chose one within my comfort zone for the first year, and set up a work placement in a mental health organisation in Bristol using voice work. I had no experience of working with mental health issues, except for my Shiatsu practice with Headway, the charity for head injuries.

My group of eight consisted mostly of men, which was a new experience for me as I usually work with women. They were anxious, uncomfortable in their bodies, and appeared not to want to be present. They displayed little facial expression, so it was difficult to sense what they were feeling, but their posture showed extremely low self-esteem, with heads looking down at the ground on slumped shoulders. I decided to teach them the simple and beautiful Six Healing Sounds Taoist practice, which works with breath, posture and movement using inner sounds to connect with the inner self and organs of the body. It can also be performed sitting in an upright chair which proved extremely useful.

The group took part enthusiastically and began to change their posture, sitting up with straight backs and heads held high. I worked with singing bowls, flute, drums and rattles and encouraged the group to have some fun playing with the instruments. We also worked with the Seven Chakra mantra with the mudras and sounds connecting to all their centres. Some got it and others didn't. The physical movements proved quite challenging for some, but they all sang and chanted as best they could. They particularly loved the drums.

During our second session the men played the drums opening into a real freedom of expression. Meanwhile, I started some free voice work and to my complete amazement they all joined in, making the most amazing free sounds - wild but contained. I was gobsmacked! With other groups I have worked with it has taken months of work to get to a place where the attendees let go with no inhibitions! Rhythm appeared to be very important to them which was why the drums proved to be such a success. We finished off with the Seven Chakra Mantra working in pairs facing one another, but it was hard for them to look at each other. The sessions really stretched me, because it was hard to facilitate, drum and sing all at the same time, as well as staying fully present with my group. However, the staff were thrilled with my sessions and reported that the group found it very helpful having a space in which they could express their emotions without words, and they certainly loved the chanting.

The work had taken me to the edge, but it was a joy to witness the positive changes in the group. I learnt that the greatest offering I could give to mental health patients was love, acceptance and listening, coupled with some fun and laughter! My tutor mirrored back to me that I must give these things to myself as well.

## ISLAM

Having visited Egypt to swim with dolphins at Sinai, I was familiar with the Call to Prayer, which haunts and calls to me. It truly awakens something within my soul, calling me to a place of connection to the Divine. I am also drawn to their practice of the Salat - the physical, mental and spiritual act of prayer which is observed five times a day at prescribed times, and have been more active myself in the discipline which regular worship requires. If I have had previous lives, I am sure one took place in Egypt, so perhaps it is not surprising that the sounds and the rituals have made such an impression on me - I know them of old.

I am challenged by the dogma and rules regarding how a Muslim must act in relation to the world, and to his belief that Allah is outside us; and that if the teachings of the Qur'an are not adhered to, then people will be judged on the Day of Judgement and punished if they have not followed the rules. I am challenged by many aspects of this religion – the belief that God is all powerful and can render us powerless if he so wishes; the belief that the Qur'an is a revelation from behind a veil of light sent through a messenger to reveal what God permits and wills; and the system of penalties which people can undertake for wrongdoings.

I am also uncomfortable with the imbalance of feminine and masculine power. Muslim men are allowed more than one wife and many women feel they have to dress by covering themselves completely. In some traditions this includes the niqab, which covers their beautiful faces, although I do honour this as a choice the women make, as an act of faith and courage. The study of Islam was like my first day of learning mathematics at school. I had no basis on which to understand this vast subject, and I still feel I am wandering in the dark.

However, the mystical sect of Islam known as Sufism fascinates me. The Sufis have a great understanding of metaphysical truths, an awareness of what brings a soul closer to the Divine and what pushes it away. At one time, I sang Sufi chants and danced with a small community of Sufis, and felt very comfortable with their aspirations. The Sufi tradition feels expansive and ecstatic.

I am still sitting with how I can address the challenge of dogma which appears in all the Abrahamic religions. The issue of right and wrong is tricky for me as my mind sees everything as it is. It just is. It is also one of the issues I have with Christianity, my original faith path.

## BUDDHISM
This is a faith path in which I had already immersed myself over a period of two years, when I became a member of a Buddhist

community (a Sangha) after my father died. I am attracted by the simplicity of the main understanding of the various traditions of Buddhism, in that they direct us to 'look within ourselves' with a willingness to find the Truth, to make up our own minds on the issue of who or what God is, and to take steps to awaken our own sense of Truth, which seems to me to be a much more universal approach. I like the teachings, which combine both rational analysis and a brilliantly clear psychological understanding of the human mind, emphasising the importance of kindness, loving intent and action, and compassion towards all beings - not just people.

Buddhism honours the truth of life on earth, and the human condition of suffering in the form of attachment to the material world and to thoughts run by our Ego mind. I like the main practice of this path, which is meditation. I believe our thoughts control our destiny, and therefore we need to quieten the busy human mind in order to observe and watch our thoughts, and thus change those which do not serve us in life. Buddha said "All we are is the result of what we have thought" and urged us to witness the power of our minds, respect its power and use it to cultivate self-knowledge, knowledge of others and a knowledge of the purpose of the world.

However, much of my own spiritual practice is body centred. Purely focussing on the mind challenges me. I prefer to go through the body to the mind and back to the body, as the body has been my messenger and teacher in life.

Buddhism, like every other religion, has many sects with different interpretations of their law, including Theravada, Mahayana and Zen, Tibetan, Tantra, and Nirchen Dirsham.

## CHRISTIANITY & THE CHURCH OF ENGLAND
One would have thought that this study would be a piece of cake for me but it was not; not for me, nor for many of the

others in the group, particularly the Irish Catholics. We were blessed with a wonderful tutor, however, a Church of England minister from Birmingham - a city where every faith is represented.

My roots lie in this faith, along with my unshakeable connection to Jesus, Mother Mary, Mary Magdalene and the Angelic Realms. As a child, these beings stood beside me, held me and guided me through life. I still feel their presence strongly and channel their energies in my healing work. I am also passionate about sacred church music, and have spent my life honouring God through music and song. It lives through me, as does the power of prayer, especially the Lord's Prayer.

However, as we all sat down in a circle that first morning, I began to shake uncontrollably. It was if I had gone into shock. It was a complete surprise to me. As the session continued, my condition worsened. I was filled with pain and emotion, as if I was carrying the pain of some enormous wound connected to this faith path, and not only for myself but for others in the group and for people worldwide. The feeling was so strong that it got to the stage where I began to sob and shake uncontrollably. The priest did not appear to be surprised. He came towards me, knelt before me on the floor, and placed his hand on my knee. At that point a wave of sound poured out of me, the sound of an animal in agony. It went on, while the priest 'held' me in the silence and presence of God until I had emptied something out, something very big and ugly. Then the priest began to speak "On behalf of the Church, I ask for your forgiveness for this wound that you have carried for so many years. I deeply apologise." A man of the cloth was kneeling before me asking for forgiveness for all that the church represented in the form of patriarchy. Many members of the group came to me afterwards to express their gratitude for what I had done on their behalf. It was the first of two major healings for me within the training, and probably the most important.

Having to do the study work gave me the opportunity to read about esoteric Christianity and the Gnostic gospels, which is what speaks to me now - the ancient path to Christ before the dogma came in. I also attended a Taizé service in a local church, which involved sung and chanted prayers, meditation, a period of silence, liturgical readings and icons, and no preaching. It was beautiful. The whole service resonated with 'my way' of following a path of Christianity. The Taizé community was founded in 1940 by Roger Louis Schutz-Marsauche (known as Brother Roger) who built a small ecumenical monastic centre in France with a strong devotion to peace and justice through prayer and meditation. Their hundred-strong community of Roman Catholic and Protestant monks is drawn from thirty countries across the world and has attracted followers worldwide, including a strong following among young people.

Meanwhile, I was encouraged by my mentor to turn towards the mirror each day to see my light, which has been an ongoing challenge. Yet I felt for the first time in my life that through this training I was getting closer to knowing what my faith path might look like. My body told me that it was clearing the ancestral memories which no longer served me, in order for me to move fully into my spiritual power and for me to recognise who I really am. God has given me a love of music and a love of the spoken word, as well as the gift of healing to share with others, and I began to reflect on how I could marry these skills with my faith path to bring them fully into a place of service.

## RETREAT
At the end of each year of our training, we were to spend five days in retreat - a culmination of all we had done together as a

group over each year. After the first year, students had a choice of whether or not to continue towards ordination. For various personal reasons, a few fell by the wayside. However, there was no question in my mind that I was destined to continue.

I felt at home as soon as I arrived at Croydon Hall, a beautiful haven of peace in that wild coastal part of north Somerset where I had done Voice training with Chloe Goodchild. Our first task was to undertake a session on forgiveness. This involved writing two letters each to our mothers, fathers and to God. The first explaining our difficult feelings towards them, and the second was to be one of love and forgiveness. During this process I realised that while I had forgiven my father, I had not yet forgiven my mother. I share these intimate letters with you in the hope that you will see how these tasks can give rise to letting issues go.

## Letter expressing difficult feelings

*Dear God,*

*I am writing to you, to share with you feelings I have around my religious upbringing and my relationship with you. There are two letters and this is the first about disappointments, resentments, sadness and other negative feelings I have surrounding my relationship with you.*

*First of all, I would like to say that my relationship with you has had an element of constancy ever since I was a child. In fact, the only time I felt you had left me was for a few hours of a very long night I had in the desert in Mexico whilst on a shamanic retreat. It was at a point where I was being asked to do something I had always resisted. As a medicine, I had been asked to walk out into the desert and pick the fruit of the desert which, through a process of ceremony, I was to inwardly digest* before making a long and arduous pilgrimage to a sacred place. This was intended to be a ceremonial cleansing. During the night when I was facing this fear head on, I cried out to you and you did not seem to be there, no one was there. I felt totally alone, abandoned. However, within an hour I heard you. You came to my assistance and directed me as you always do to have the courage to make this pilgrimage whatever my resistance, telling me it would be the making of me in some way, which of course it was.

I want to go back to a period of time when I was a part of the Christian church. I was being educated at a Catholic convent and my family were worshipping in the Church of England, where I was a member of the choir, a brownie and a girl guide. I was being taught about the ethics of life in a strong way both by my parents and 'the church'. I was taught that I was to 'obey authority', other people's authority, and that I was a child of sin, filled with shame and guilt. When I think about this now I feel angry because my own integrity as a human being was dishonoured through this process. The belief in my sin gave me very low self-esteem, and my personal power was taken away from me. It was within this religious dogma, coupled with support from my parents, that I learnt to 'fear' you instead of 'love' you. You were at the time looking down on me from above and deciding whether I was worthy of heaven, or whether I was to be punished by going to hell. It left me very confused and unhappy, with feelings of never being good enough.

It wasn't until I became ill at the age of forty that I realised what I had learnt about you and 'authority'. I knew then that I had to search for the God inside me, to learn to connect with that part of me that was LOVE and LIGHT; the part that was whole, full of integrity, compassion and empathy. I have made a long journey over twenty years to discover who I really am.

*It is through the eastern religions and traditions of this
world, that I have seen 'the light' and left the darkness behind,
the darkness in which I had been enveloped for some twenty
years of my adult life.*

*I even thought that I had to 'obey' my first husband,
which the marriage vows at the time insisted we made. For
another twenty years I did just that, well, for much of the
time. I swallowed my own needs in order to attend to his.
And let go of my own identity, my own personal authority.*

*I feel sadness about the amount of my life which has been
in the darkness and the shadow which has manifested in the
physical deterioration of my body, and I now revel in being
so much more in my Light now.*

*I forgive these people as "they knew not what they did",
and I am in the process of forgiving myself for going along
with it all, and giving away my personal power. I know that
it is my soul path, that I was put on this earth to experience
this as my destiny. It has been painful.*

*Now at the age of sixty, the Christian story as in the King
James Version of the Bible, is a source of some doubt. I feel
warmer to the stories within the gnostic gospels. I believe
Jesus was a mystic himself, and of course we need to remind
ourselves that he was not a Christian but a Jew. He was a
healer and one of the many masters, along with Buddha, and
Muhammad, and Krishna. I feel saddened that women have
been dishonoured within these faith paths. I am sad that the
transcendental element of the Christian religion has meant
that it has lost touch with the feminine, the mystical, the
connection with the earth and its elements; it has lost its
spirituality in exchange for dogma. I feel it has lost its heart.*

*As a result, I am passionate about a changing world and
assisting its process in healing these areas. I represent the
mystical arenas and I feel such sadness when I witness the*

*wars and the conflict caused by religious extremism. I want to be a part of a change on this earth, whereby people reconnect with the earth, with their spirituality and their wholeness.*

*With undying love, Hilary*

## My Love letter to God

*Beloved God,*

*My heart cries out for the ultimate form - to know you without the trappings of my human conditioning, without anything which gets in the way of this relationship with you. I want to know your presence in every moment of my life. I do not need a religion to do this. I just need to make friends with my shadow and hear the sound of your heartbeat, your voice to direct me. I know that I am getting closer to this state of being than I have been in the past and I am aware of the further steps I have to take along that path.*

*I acknowledge my human self in the world and I am learning how to be the light that I am in the world. Your presence does now sit within me, and yet still my humanness falls back into the trap of fear sometimes. I want to be able to acknowledge my relationship with you within my circle of family and friends, and to be open about this with them instead of hiding it away. Something scares me about being truly open about who you are and who I am and that we are one and the same. People have been mocked for such an understanding. How can I be more open about this precious relationship in my life? Maybe this ministry training is going to help me overcome my God shyness and allow me to share the beauty of it with others.*

*I can see by writing these letters that my relationship with you in my early years was bound up with limitations. Now it is becoming my route to freedom, my route to authenticity, to integrity, to becoming who I am, my own master...oh that feels truly great. I want to celebrate this relationship and what I can see is that my ordination will be a sacred marriage between my human self and my true self, with God. What a joy that will be. So I am preparing myself and working on my own self-forgiveness so that I can surely be emptied out and filled up with the light of who you are and who I am.*

*That then will be the beginning of another new chapter, walking in the world in the Light of God.*

*In your abiding presence, Hilary*

**INITIATION**

The ceremonial space had been prepared in the Great Hall and all we students were lined up outside, dressed in ceremonial white. There was a sense of anticipation, but we had no idea as to what was going to happen next. Our mentors invited us into the space to undergo a purification ritual, so we entered the Hall, where the Faculty Staff were waiting, to the strains of "A Hundred Thousand Angels" - one of my favourite tracks from the Danish band, Bliss. Feelings of bliss arose within me and I immediately began to blub, before anything had even happened! We worked in pairs, washing each other's feet from a bowl of sacred water - a beautiful healing process of great love performed in silence, accompanied by the gentle sound of Bliss. It was such a moving experience.

The faculty staff and mentors approached us individually, asking if we wished to take part in the initiation. As each assented, they placed a 'first year' stole around our necks and blessed us with LOVE. I felt myself melting into who I am; something fell away from me in that moment. I had lost my resistance and had given myself to the OneSpirit, God - whoever or whatever God is.

During this first year of training a great deal had taken place. I had received a necessary repair to my left hip which had enabled me to walk easily again; had made a Pilgrimage to Chartres; and had enjoyed sisterhood within two groups I was facilitating. My beautiful second grandchild, Liliana Blossom, had come into the world, and although she had had a difficult start due to breathing problems, she was allowed home after ten days to be cared for and welcomed into the family by my daughter Celia and her husband. I had also spent a very special time with Celia around the birth and afterwards. I felt solid in my relationship with Norm as he seemed to be a part of my training, by proxy, due to his interest in knowing of a greater power and yet knowing that religion was not his path. When I set about my homework, we would have world view discussions which somehow deepened our relationship and stimulated my own understanding of a changing world view.

## SECOND YEAR MINISTRY

After a short break over August, the second year began. I was excited, because an important element of what drew me to the training in the first place was the Art of Ceremony (a form of which I was already using in my work as a facilitator). We would be encouraged to develop public speaking, an activity which has always taken me to the edge of terror! We would be looking into the power of Prayer and Meditation, studying William Bloom's approach to Modern Spirituality. We would need to organise our second work placement. Finally, each of us would create a Vow as an anchor to our ministry, one which we would use every day of our lives to support ourselves and our work.

To be able to step further into awakening, oneness and service, the Ceremonies and Ritual part of the course demanded that we look at the emotional aspects of relationships. We were tasked with creating and ministering ceremonies covering all the rites of passage - birth, adolescence, marriage, and death - to be shared and witnessed within our small study group, followed by a group discussion of each experience. We were to face, examine and process: trauma and its consequences; recovery from trauma; death, dying and bereavement; depression and joy; anger and grief. It was necessary for us to face the extremities of our feelings before being allowed to conduct ceremonies with others, within which any or all of these emotions might arise. This would be a major commitment, necessitating an extra day each month - a huge amount of work, even greater than the previous year.

Dealing with my birth occasioned the second major healing of my Ministry training. Our Faculty leader was very experienced in the subject, with a great deal of knowledge about the awareness infants have at birth. She explained that it is a crucial moment when we all make up our minds about the world we are encountering - whether or not it is a safe environment and whether or not it feels welcoming. These fundamental feelings at birth remain with us and can inform our world view as adults. As we sat in the group circle listening to her explain that a great deal of trauma can occur around our physical and spiritual birth, I began to shake, just as I had done in the session on Christianity. Shake so violently that I briefly stopped breathing. Just before I was about to pass out I heard my mentor, Nicola, exhorting me to "Breathe, Hilary, breathe!" Emotional, tearful and weak, I felt exhausted and extremely vulnerable throughout the whole of the following week. In my one-to-one counselling session with my mentor, she encouraged me to view my grief as an opportunity to expand into LOVE, and we set about uncovering the underlying cause of my distress.

It emerged that my soul had been frightened to be on this

earth; that I had not felt that sufficient love had been involved in drawing me here - that the intent had not been deep enough. I therefore had great resistance in leaving my divine heaven, or leaving the womb and was fearful of treading this earth which felt harsh and unwelcoming. There was a place within that needed to be honoured, soothed and comforted. We also reviewed the difficult events around the births of my own two children and that of my grandchildren, and it was glaringly obvious that I needed to release unhelpful ancestral patterns around birthing.

I spent the month preparing a rebirthing ceremony for myself 'to honour the soul which was resistant to come in.' This took place in the bosom of my study group with fellow student minister and experienced Shamanic & Ancestral Practitioner, Maura Clesham, facilitating the process for me, culminating in my being renamed Hilary Eliza.

## WORK PLACEMENT

Having worked with emotionally challenged individuals the previous year, it occurred to me that perhaps I could be of service working within a hospital environment. The local hospital in Bath agreed to take me on. There was a sense of reticence from the other ministers as they had been used to dealing with Anglican ministers and it was the first time that they had worked with an Interfaith member who would be working from a slightly different ethos, but in the main I was welcomed warmly. The work on the wards principally involved allaying people's fears as I visited, talked and prayed with them. Some talked of their impending deaths and some of their relationship with God. However, I learnt that the hospital system seemed to have little concept of 'accompanying' people in death. It was distressing to find a dying man left quite alone. I realised how much people close to death need someone else's presence, reassurance and holding. I also observed how different cultures have different needs at this time. It was good experience.

## MY VOW

In the spring, we began work on preparing our individual Vows. We were advised to give it time to grow and develop, as a seed grows into a plant. By early summer mine had become a plant, rooted deep in my consciousness.

We were guided to:

- Consider expanding into a position of leadership
- Review our connection with the Divine
- Look at the deepest untruth about old lifetime patterns that no longer serve us, and then turn that untruth around.

To do this I began looking at the issue of TRUTH. Since the truth was not always seen or spoken of during my childhood, it was important for me to honour Truth:

"I Vow to uphold the Spirit of Truth and Unity."

I had only recently rediscovered my Authority and it is still sometimes a challenge for me to claim it:

"I Vow to stand in my Authority."

I wanted to rise above JUDGEMENT, both of myself and others:

"I Vow to see the divine in all beings." (all people)

Those unhealthy patterns can then be turned around by speaking this vow rather like a mantra each day of my life reminding me of the areas where I need to pay attention: Truth, Authority, Judgement:

"I Vow to uphold the Spirit of Truth and Unity."

"I Vow to stand in my own Authority."

"I Vow to see the divine in all beings."

## Truth

Feel the soft earth beneath your feet
And touch the soul of beauty
Feel yourself before me
Listen to your voice
God is in the breath
The Breath is in God
Breathe through soft sounds
Hear the echoes of your heart
Feel the love of your soul
Hear the sound of the drum
Rhythms in the bones
Stroke the soft skin of your body
Utter whispers of love
Speak quietly in hushed whispers
Oh magnificent beauty that you are
Sing that song again, the one which
Speaks of your magnificence
Swaying like the branches of the trees
So then the body moves in synchronicity
With everything all at once
Stop. Stand still. Stop right here.
It is perfect just now.
Just now is perfection.
Stamp out, bang the drum of time
Until all can hear it
Send out your message to the earth
It will be heard.
Speak clearly what you have to say and let others hear
Crack open the shell for all to see and hear
It is the TRUTH
No one can deny it,
It is the truth, the truth, the truth.

*Hilary Eliza Franklin*

Rather like a thesis at the end of a degree, we were also asked to prepare a manual demonstrating our creativity and passion and uniqueness, to include the ceremonies, poems, songs and prayers which we had created over the past two years, complete with our mission statement and personal vow. I wrote:

"I am thrilled to begin this manual to celebrate the completion of my training. My whole life to this point has been a pilgrimage and journey towards this moment in time. All that I have learnt is bringing me into service as a minister. So the service of ordination is a gift to myself for all the energy and work I have put in throughout my life, and particularly since I awoke to the realisation that I was responsible for what course my health, my wellbeing, my spirituality and physicality would take. So it is with great joy that I commit myself to service within my community, directed by the God within me to do this work always with the awareness and consciousness that self-care comes first; then care of my family; and finally care of others."

During the course of my training, I received healing in two particular areas of my life - my religious wounding, and my birth and entry into the world. The work around our shadow and resistances has led me to a place of forgiveness. That shadow aspect of ourselves which we refuse to love demonstrates that it is a call for LOVE. If we do not forgive ourselves, the whole world is against us. The shadow is the fear of letting go of our guilt, but forgiveness frees us from guilt and shame, and liberates both our relationships and our lives.

## ORDINATION

During the final month of training, we prepared for our ordination ceremony with another five-day retreat, again at Croydon Hall, which was to include the Vow Ceremony, a private, intimate ceremony witnessed only by Ministers. For me it was the ultimate sacred union, a commitment to my soul as a union of the inner and outer God surrendering myself to a life of Service. Two days after that I was ordained as a One Spirit Interfaith Minister in London, witnessed by my husband, children, grandchildren, brother and sister-in-law, another sister-in-law and several special friends. I was elated. We had a marvellous party afterwards at a Tapas restaurant in Notting Hill.

---

### RESOURCES

One Spirit Interfaith Foundation and Seminary
www.interfaithfoundation.org

The Healing of Birth - a film by Elmer Postle,
Fonix Musik & Ficon, Denmark

---

Chapter Fifteen

# CEREMONY AND SPIRITUAL COUNSELLING

*"Ceremony is typically magical, creative and healing, and provides a bridge between the material and the spirit worlds. It's a felt demonstration of how the power of the universe works, and it provides an excellent way to honour all those events in our lives that we want to sanctify."*

Steven D Farmer, PhD

CEREMONY HAS BEEN weaving itself into my life for some years now, but it was not until I began Ministerial training that I realised the fullness of its strength. It has the power to heal, the power to change people's lives and in particular, relationships. No matter the stated purpose of a ceremony, it inevitably helps heal a fundamental spiritual wound - the illusion of separateness from the Creator and Creation. By our participation in ceremony, we are reassured that we are not independent from that which sustains us materially and spiritually. We are reminded of our place within the vast and intricate network of life.

Ceremonies touch people's hearts and that is their great magic. Ceremony gives our inner wisdom a place and time to emerge and take form. Ceremonies are principally targeted toward transitions or celebrations, and for special events they give meaning to the transition itself. What better way is there of commemorating important events such as marriage, personal achievements and anniversaries than to join with others in joyous and sacred celebration?

Creating a sacred ritual is a wonder-filled way to honour the cycles of life, a vehicle to support the flow of our lives, just as a rose is a vehicle to support the bee. For the bee to develop, the rose has a particular form and function in delivering nectar to fulfil and nourish the life of the bee. I am passionate about honouring the natural rhythms of our Great Mother Earth, such as the change of seasons or the monthly arrival of the full moon, although many of our religions have forgotten to honour our Great Mother, the Divine Feminine, through the witnessing of nature's cycles. I also believe that we can bring even greater richness to our religious and cultural holidays by employing elements of ceremony.

There are three different types of ceremony - Healing, Transition and Celebration - each of which is structured like a story to include a beginning, middle and end, the main highlight taking place in the middle. My experience is that the simpler the plan, the more powerful it is. It is also important that every aspect has a reason, so that it doesn't distract from the main purpose. The central climax of every ceremony - the moment when everyone is totally aware and 'present' and something greater than us materialises - is when inner shifts and subconscious changes can happen, beyond words and beyond form.

My place as a minister is to celebrate the uniqueness of everyone's intentions, and as a result no two ceremonies are the same. Focussing on the needs of the people who come to me, I always create something unique, and the power of that ceremony comes through that authentic process. The same applies to services of worship. It is the focus and clarity with which we set the intention together, in the presence of the One Spirit, the Divine, that gives the ceremony of worship such power. There is also the mystical dimension of having two or more people gathered together which creates a greater sense of connection, both on a Divine and a social level.

A ceremony may be intended for a specific healing, such as relieving suffering, be it emotional, physical, or spiritual; or we may call for spiritual assistance through ceremony to repair relationships; or to mitigate some situation in our community. Ceremonies are often clothed in particular customs of religion or race or culture, but they do not need to be. With an open heart and a clear intention, you can develop ceremonies for yourself, your family and your community. I am particularly drawn to facilitating unique, creative, bespoke ceremonies for individuals, family and community, drawing on guidance from Spirit and with the co-operation of the enhanced, powerful and mysterious forces of Life.

Since my ordination, I have had much opportunity to be of Service. My dear friend Patsy's daughter, Jasmine, was diagnosed with terminal cancer aged just thirty-eight. She wanted to know how I had healed myself and so triggered me into beginning this book. She was a beautiful young woman, an artist who painted mystical creatures, dolphins and eagles in bright, light acrylic colours, yet she was stricken with some internalised grief. I was called to support both her and her mother as she moved toward her death in December 2013. Jasmine always had hopes of getting better, at no time accepting that death was going to happen, even towards the very end.

I could not imagine how I was going to have the courage or the emotional strength to take her funeral, yet somehow I was given all that was necessary. My friend chose a chapel for the funeral which had no particular religious association and we filled it with Jasmine's paintings, flowers and many, many candles. A mutual friend and professional cellist and healer, Linda Stocks, played music with incredible reverence, musicality and passion. Jasmine's sister, father and mother spoke, as did a cousin who also played a song Jasmine had written. If funerals can be beautiful, it was beautiful, and we felt her presence. We each placed a rose upon her coffin before we took our leave of her for the last time.

Being just six months after my ordination, it was a huge milestone for me, but as ministers we also have earthly help to guide us through these journeys - an important aspect of our profession. Rev. Nicola Aven, my mentor, often fulfils that role for me, alongside my Supervisor, Rev. Jean Farrell, both of whom saw me through my ministerial training. The universe works in truly strange and magnificent ways, for within two days of the funeral I took my first wedding ceremony. It was for a beautiful couple who had worked with me in preparation for their marriage. They had gained much clarity and understanding through examining their spiritual beliefs, their wounds and their plans for having a family. As I write, I have just heard that we will soon be celebrating a Blessing and Naming Ceremony for their first child. So you can see what a beautiful job I have.

## My Ceremonies

### 1. Blessings and Namings

In the OneSpirit Interfaith practice, this is equivalent to a Baptism in the Church of England, and is for the purpose of consciously sanctifying the entrance of a soul into the world, so that the person may walk through life remembering their true essence as a part of God; to give thanks for the miracle of new life; to support the mother and father in stepping into parenthood consciously with love and clarity; to acknowledge the sacred role that the grandparents and godparents hold; and to honour mutual connection.

2. *Rite of Passage in Adolescence*
This ceremony is a cross-cultural phenomenon. Adolescence is often a time of turmoil and can be assisted with right intentions from elders. These rituals have existed throughout human history and can be a significant factor in the development of a stable adult personality. This type of ritual has been lost in our Western Christian culture and one of my longings is that it be brought back, particularly to help young women as they reach womanhood. This rite usually requires the candidate to be separated from society, then to receive instruction from an elder before being welcomed back into society with acknowledgement of the adolescent's changed status. The ceremony generally includes a spiritual cleansing, offerings, prayers and blessings with traditional food and music.

3. *Marriages and Unions within Relationships*
Many people are now seeking a ceremony outside the restrictions of a particular faith. Some desire a spiritual ceremony whilst others do not. Couples of differing faiths or same sex couples can be assisted within the OneSpirit Interfaith work.

4. *Death, Funerals and Memorials*
Nowadays, many people prepare their own funeral so that it is handled in a way that resonates with their life and personality, and because it saves the family entering into difficult discussions and arguments about how to handle a ceremony at a time of grief and shock.

5. *Release Ceremonies and Healing Ceremonies*
Ceremonies for release of relationships and personal healing for illness.

Just as it is important to honour the joining of people in marriage, so it is equally important when couples decide that their relationship cannot continue, they take the step consciously. Honouring one another for what has been by expressing gratitude for what has been good, and expressing sorrow, anger and regret for what has not worked, facilitates a separation that comes from a place of acceptance and love without resentment. This ceremony comes into the category of healing, as an enormous amount of healing takes place within the closure of a relationship when it is performed consciously. The ideal situation is when both partners come together to accomplish this. However, it is possible to create a ceremony with just one partner working at an energetic level to release the other so that vows that bind and rings that bind can be released. When people are marrying for a second time, it is good to release from a previous marriage before making the new vows.

Healing ceremonies also take place within my one-to-one spiritual counselling work to release emotional issues. The client holds an intention for his/herself to release a situation in their life which is causing emotional difficulties and then brings in an intention to create something new in its place. Letting go ceremonies work particularly well at full moon, while bringing in new intentions are best conducted at new moon.

## THE POWER OF SPIRITUAL COUNSELLING
The power of the skills learnt as a spiritual counsellor has seen me through the past two years of sitting with my mother and her developing dementia in her care home. It has required a

non-judgemental listening, a complete acceptance of her own understanding of where she is in her story, even it was not real for me, and without any need for me to receive what I might have needed as her daughter. In Naked Voice terms - the power of the witness and loyal friend 'in action'.

Spiritual Counselling is a way of being with someone in the spirit of love, equality and friendship with an awareness of the Presence of the Divine - the counsellor acting as a spiritual bridge. Internally, spiritual counselling is an activity of the heart, where we extend energetically the grace and direct knowledge which we receive in our own spiritual life, and offer that to meet the need of another. It is linked in with witnessing of which I have spoken in Chapter Ten, in that it is completely non-judgemental and incorporates the skill of deep listening, with no agenda or intention other than to allow intuition and the presence of LOVE to lead the process.

It can come in the form of counselling, the facilitation of group work, or interlaced with ceremony. It is a 'listening' and 'holding' activity. It supports both counsellor and client in accepting and letting go of unconscious storylines based on guilt, fear and lack, and instead supports the truth of who we are, loving, whole and at one with all life. It is a form of awakening: out of our fearful self-images, to experience and accept our inherent wholeness; out of our fearful projections of other people, to see them as inherently whole no matter what mistakes they have made; out of our fearful perceptions of the world, and our sense of being a victim in that world; and finally, out of a mind-set of separation, into the depth of our oneness with all beings.

As a counsellor, it is my work to enable my clients to access and use the inner resources they already have, with the intention of loving them back into the awareness of who they are.

One of the greatest joys I have in this realm is when I am preparing a couple for marriage. I enable them to access thoughts and feelings about their intentions for their relationship which they may not have shared with one another, and I get them to speak to one another of these intentions in my presence as the witness. Couples readily acknowledge what a profound experience it is to be able to dig down to a deeper level of understanding, speak their thoughts out loud and have a witness in that speaking.

Equally, when I am preparing for a funeral or memorial, it is my role to enable people to speak not only of the wonderful picture they have of their loved ones, but also of the facets of the deceased which were perhaps difficult, or even wrought havoc in the family dynamics. It can be a very healing process to voice these within the body of the funeral ceremony, enabling members of the family to be real in the sharing of their memory of the deceased. This is a powerful healing that can be addressed within ceremony, which is why at times there is no line to draw between ceremony and spiritual counselling.

Before I begin any form of counselling I am clear with the client about the length of time we will spend together and what the cost of the session may be, usually set according to their means. The space in which I work is always blessed and the room set up mindfully so that it is as relaxing, calming, clean, comfortable and as aesthetically pleasing as possible. I align myself internally through preparation exercises; open to the Source of all LOVE, and open to feel and connect with whatever that person is experiencing, which helps dissolve the client's feeling of being alone in their pain, which is healing in itself. I hold firm to the knowledge that although their pain is certainly the truth of their experience, it is not the truth of their being, so I am extending my empathy on a human level whilst internally denying the reality of the fear, guilt and shame which my client presents to me. Thus I am meeting my client where they believe themselves to be, and where they truly are as eternally whole within God. This helps create a psychic bridge upon which the client can come to see the unreality of their own fears and thus begin to let them go.

To maintain this work, my personal ethic is a continual development of myself in order to extend love and support to others. This calls me to surrender even more to a deepening of my own spiritual practice.

I love my work now with a passion.

---

### RESOURCES

One Spirit Interfaith Foundation and Seminary
www.interfaithfoundation.org

---

Chapter Sixteen

# A GLOBAL PEACE
# THROUGH SPIRITUALITY

*"A spirituality that is only private and self-absorbed, one
devoid of an authentic political and social consciousness,
does little to halt the suicidal juggernaut of history.
When the deepest and most grounded spiritual vision is
married to a practical and pragmatic drive to transform
all existing political, economic, and social institutions,
a holy force – the power of wisdom and love in action –
is born."*

Andrew Harvey, Author, scholar and
teacher of mystic traditions

THE COMPLETION OF this book is the opening of the next
doorway for me, and maybe for you as the reader. It is
an invitation for you and I to go deeper. It has catalysed my
own awareness of the next step in my consciousness. I feel I
have taken care of the ground work, and built the mechanism
for being a conduit for the Source of all Life. I can now move
into receiving a greater and more profound awareness of what
it is to be on this earth as this conduit. Being a conduit enables
me to know and love who I am, and yet my sense is that this is
merely the beginning of a greater understanding.

I am on the cusp of something new - I have a dream and I
believe it is not just my dream, but the dream of many – a dream
of a global peace and understanding. As our consciousness is

elevating, so there will be a realisation that our individual understanding of who or what God is can take any form, a knowing that there is only one SOURCE with many pathways toward that ONE SOURCE. The purpose of this dream is that everyone on earth will understand their connection with all that is, enabling us to live in harmony with our earthly treasures - the land, the oceans, the skies - and with one another as human beings, knowing we are all interconnected. With this understanding peace can prevail. We will live in our innate joy and be 'Love in Action'.

I offer myself in service to that dream knowing that I will be called upon to respond, and to join with others who are dreaming similar dreams. Just as my pilgrimages have shown, we don't need to know what is around the corner, merely to trust that by following our hearts, guidance will come. We simply need to take one step forward, then listen, waiting for the next step to beckon.

It is hopefully evident from reading this story that my mask has slowly and gradually fallen away, leaving me with more clarity about how to go about life, with a deep understanding that the universe of life guides us, if we do but listen. In particular it has encompassed a series of lessons within relationships highlighting the significance of balancing both masculine and feminine. The design for my Minister's 'stole' (the symbolic ceremonial garment denoting my dedication to service) embodies this idea. Highly coloured on a background of gold silk it has flames flaring up the right side representing the masculine, and drops of water falling down the left side, representing the feminine.

I am left with a passion for understanding how we can bring about a vital balance between masculine and feminine on this earth. John Gray, the relationship counsellor who wrote 'Men are from Mars, Women are from Venus' - that legendary guide that mothers recommend to their daughters, friends give as gifts, and brothers steal from their sisters - urges that until we balance our male and female energies there will continue to be an unbreachable gulf between the powerful and the powerless.

Andrew Harvey has the best way I know of describing it when he says:

*"The one hope for the future lies, I believe, in Sacred Activism – the fusion of the deepest spiritual knowledge and passion with clear, wise, radical action in all the arenas of the world, inner and outer. We have very little time in which to awaken and transform ourselves, to be able to preserve the planet, and to heal the divisions between the powerful and the powerless. Let us go forward now with firm resolve and profound dedication."*

There are large groups of people from many differing walks of life who are becoming activists, envisioning a new world in which we can choose to follow our hearts and our passions; where we don't have to 'fit into the system' and follow the indoctrination of the media; where we take care of and honour our great Mother Earth; nourishing our families and communities and changing the separatism which has arisen in our western world; where we are free to believe what we wish; bring up our children as we wish; where we feed ourselves on locally grown food where possible, take responsibility for our environment, our health, our lives and one another; where we love and provide for our children's creativity and emotional wellbeing so well that they don't need fixing as adults, and can in turn raise generations of well-adjusted human beings where peace may reign.

It feels as if the time has come to renew our understanding of community, let go of separateness, and gather together consciously including the legal, commercial, financial, political, medical, religious and social institutions. The crises in our world today are in themselves calls to action, opportunities to rally together and achieve a different paradigm - a peaceful and sustainable planet. The first step is to begin with ourselves, by peeling away our masks to raise self-confidence and self-belief. Through renewing our passions and tapping into and stimulating our creativity we can feel empowered to take action and become inspired, effective and practical agents of institutional and systemic change.

I see many receiving this call and responding to it in their own individual way, both in my generation and in my children's generation. This call to change is exciting. As a result of our INTERCONNECTION, when we change the magic of the energy that links us all brings about change in everyone around us. In healing ourselves we not only serve this generation but the next and the next. This understanding has been enough to drive me onwards through times when it has all felt a little too much. Great help is at hand, from healers, ministers and counsellors to support those whose courage enables them to say 'yes' to personal change.

Whether the call comes from the mind - dissatisfaction with a life situation, depression or addiction - or from the body through some form of illness, it is our responsibility to awaken to the call. All we have to do is step out of that familiar groove and follow our hearts. The unknown can be scary, but soldiering on wearing a mask is not the answer. Perhaps my story will help you to appreciate just what gifts and rewards can result when one steps forward, even into fear and uncertainty. Release those limiting thoughts, beliefs and behavior and trust that a new way of being awaits.

## ACTIVISM IN ACTION WITHIN THE FAMILY
When my thirty-nine-year-old son Alexander became severely depressed, it was his wake-up call to become more true to himself. With the support of family and a 'Human Givens' Coach, he got back on his feet quite quickly. During his coaching, he experienced a light bulb moment when he clearly

envisioned what he wanted to do "with his one wild and precious life". Within two months, he had attracted a new partner who is the love of his life, and taken steps toward fulfilling his passion. I am so inspired by what he is doing that I asked him if he would share it with you as it so clearly demonstrates that, first and foremost, life is what you make it...

*"I spent nearly 40 years of my life 'wearing a mask' trying to fit into a life of money, not making a life of my own, but letting the past control my future. Society wants to airbrush us and I, like many, allowed it to happen to me. Why should so many of us become ill to realise we must take off our masks and go for life? Do what we love.*

*"Many of us spend so long reaching for a happiness we will never find; constantly aiming for the next goal; saving for the next holiday; or the next house; or car. In this process, yes, we will have peaks of happiness as we reach each goal, but is it true happiness? My experience is that very shortly after each goal is achieved we plateau until we reach the next need. When will we stop and realise that happiness is all the little things that happen every day? It's a hug from a loved one, a smile from a new friend or a sunny day.*

*"No-one ever won an award for being average. We don't wake up in the morning and think 'I'm going to be average today!' and yet that is precisely what many of us spend our life doing. It's time for a revolution. It's time for a movement.* Transition *is a choice.* Growth *is a choice and my calling is to inspire and help people to go all in and commit to saying 'I don't fit in...I'm going for it.' To help people break through their fear of change, and the focus on money-making, because they fear they are not going to have enough.*

*"I am starting a movement by working one-to-one to inspire and help one hundred people to find what they love, go for it*

*and make a sustainable living from it. I believe in the power and use of Story and that the best way to empower people to commit to change and to do what they love, is by connecting them with people who have already achieved that; people who have proved that life becomes exciting, a place to flourish and find happiness, by doing something in which they truly believe.*

*"This movement is spreading fast through word-of-mouth and as it builds so does a community of ambassadors to help the movement grow across the world. I am already half-way through helping the 100 make this transition. Their personal stories are epic, so I am going to make short films to share online, creating a global platform which will give thousands and millions of people the tools to find and do what they love; break through the fear of change; and go 'all in' on life. Watch this space...!"*

*Alex Brenan*

If you believe in synchronicity, just one year later, almost to the day, my daughter Celia was struck down with severe anxiety. She had been raising a family in conjunction with a career in Social Work in a city centre for some sixteen years when her supervisor began to press her to take the next step up the career ladder. The stress this engendered was insupportable. She has since given up this career, moved out of the City into a seaside location with her husband and family. I know this move will allow her to take off the mask she has worn to protect herself in that environment for so long, and become her creative, joyful, wise mother self.

My stepson Christopher received a wake-up call when he became seriously ill in his forties after several stressful years working in a blue chip company. The illness inspired him and his partner of ten years to create a simpler, more balanced way of living that suited both their personal and professional lives.

They devised a four-day work week which allows them to spend three days doing what they love - spending time with their dogs, horses and sheep in rural Dorset. They are both thriving and flourishing, appreciating every moment of their new life.

I honour each of them and their partners in their quest to remove the mask and stop 'fitting in'. Meanwhile, my brother and I are still enjoying the company of our mother, who through her dementia has learnt to receive love and care, and as a result is somehow more at peace, despite the dementia. I also feel that my father is ready in the wings to take good care of her when she does surrender herself to the Light, and it is my promise to her that I shall midwife her along the way.

After more than twenty years of good use, my first hip replacement has been revised (the plastic cup in which the ball lay had completely worn away!). So with two bionic hips and a healthy body I am stepping forward with intent onto the next phase of my path. Norman and I have moved to a house that sits up high on the side of the Kennet and Avon Canal at Devizes in Wiltshire, which has brought us close to the World Heritage Site of Avebury. This Neolithic henge monument is one of the best known prehistoric sites in Britain and contains the largest stone circle in Europe. It is both a tourist attraction and a place of ancient religious importance to contemporary Druids and Pagans. Although I am not a Druid or a Pagan, I am interested in the power of these stones and the land upon which they sit, and feel blessed by their proximity and mighty presence.

If you gain anything from this book, it might be a renewed understanding that God represents Her/His Self through all life; through us as humans; through animals, trees and plants; through the land, oceans and stars; through the whole of the universe; and that we are all part of the ONE WHOLE, THE ONE SPIRIT, interconnected. To honour all of life is to honour ourselves, because everything we think and do affects the whole. We are the creative expression of the Divine. The Divine is experiencing the world through our creative expression. It seems to be a two-way field, both giving and receiving.

As one spirit, we can ask ourselves - what is LOVE? How many of us on this planet question ourselves about love? We are all an aspect of this LOVE. It is Universal. If my illness was the absence of LOVE, my recovery was the discovery of LOVE, and the CONNECTION to myself and to you. We are all part of one unified field of consciousness.

I am in awe of what happens when we surrender and trust. The Universe wants us to take off our masks and be who we truly are, to be at peace with ourselves, to love one another, to love what we are doing and to take very good care of our Mother, the Earth.

I trust in my dream.

---

### RESOURCE

Andrew Harvey is a prolific author and two books I
recommend are:
'The Return of the Mother' and 'The Hope'
www.sacredactivism.com

---

**MY PRAYER FOR YOU:**

May you know
human nature is Divine
May hope guide you
May wisdom illumine you
May the blessings
of courage and strength
be with you
and
May you find the way to

## PEEL AWAY YOUR MASK

to be true to who you really are
Blessed be

# GLOSSARY

**Connection/Interconnection**
When we feel connection it means we do not feel separated from anyone or anything. We feel part of the whole.

**Deep Listening - see Witness**

**Empath**
A person with a highly developed intuition, sensitivity, and feeling who even absorbs the emotions of others. Empaths pick up on atmospheres, can read and feel people and situations. They are heart centred nurturers who often operate as counsellors and healers.

**LOVE/ God /Presence / Source / I AM**
All capitalised LOVE refers to the LOVE that God is, LOVE itself. These are all one and the same depending on your understanding

**Intimacy**
Feeling seen and heard by another; seeing and listening to the other with honesty and truth; enjoying a soul connection; pleasure; surrender; and sensuality.

**Loyal Friend**
One who listens and does what is needed to support another without judgement.

## The Light

The supreme power / energy which is moving this whole earth, planet and universe. The light has the same significance in spirituality that the sun has in sustenance of life on this earth. Without spiritual light the darkness of ignorance can never be dispelled, and once the darkness of ignorance is removed through light of self-realisation it leads to eternal liberation.

## Mudras

Ritual Hindu / Buddhist positions of the body that have some kind of influence on the energies of the body, or your mood. Mostly the hands and fingers are held in some position, but the whole body may be part of the mudra as well. The most well-known mudras are probably the ones performed while meditating.

## Sacred Space

A space into which we enter within ourselves to discover who we are.
Or an external space cleansed and prepared for sacred work.

## Shadow

The shadow usually consists of unacknowledged negative traits, characteristics that people may be ashamed of, or deny, while they can see them clearly in others, such as carelessness, cowardice, envy, egotism, greed, materialism etc.

## Soul-Self / True-Self / Higher-Self / Light

We are all Light.
In musical language the unchanging note which lies within each of us.

## Spirituality

The acknowledgment of, and trust in, a power greater than the self.